HEINEMANN
SCHOOL
MANAGEMENT

Your School and the Law

NEIL ADAMS

Heinemann Educational
A division of Heinemann Publishers (Oxford) Ltd,
Halley Court, Jordan Hill, Oxford OX2 8EJ

OXFORD LONDON EDINBURGH
MADRID ATHENS BOLOGNA PARIS
MELBOURNE SYDNEY AUCKLAND SINGAPORE TOKYO
IBADAN NAIROBI HARARE GABORONE
PORTSMOUTH NH (USA)

First published 1992

92 93 94 95 96 10 9 8 7 6 5 4 3 2 1

A catalogue record for this book is available from the British Library on request

ISBN 0 435 80040 X

Typeset by Taurus Graphics, Kidlington, Oxon
Printed in Great Britain by Clays Ltd, St Ives plc

Acknowledgements
The author and publishers would like to thank the following for permission to reproduce copyright material: Controller of HMSO; Derbyshire Local Education Authority; School Journeys Association

Contents

Preface

Public and political interest in schools and the resulting legislation have combined to make the task of those who manage schools, whether governors, heads or assistant staff, more complicated and difficult. Governors are conscious of their responsibilities, teachers and parents aware of their rights and Heads more accountable to others. All this means that a knowledge of how the law works and an awareness of its particular application to the running of schools is essential for those who have to make important or routine decisions. I hope that this book makes their task easier.

The law discussed here is that relating to England and Wales and, mainly also, to Northern Ireland. Scottish law is based on a different system and is beyond the scope of this book. Nevertheless, much of what is said here does apply to Scotland through separate similar enactments but Scottish readers should be careful not to assume that this is so. My intentions are to help readers understand the process of law so that when changes occur they are able to put them in context; to relate the law to problems that are likely to arise in schools and suggest possible solutions; to provide assurance and certainty where that is possible and to suggest ways in which further help might be found. I have tried to avoid giving details of aspects liable to frequent change.

I spent nearly 40 years working in schools, 26 of them as a head of secondary schools, and am now Chair of Governors of a primary school. Most of the situations dealt with here are based upon my own experiences and those of friends and colleagues. I am grateful to those who have contributed to those experiences, either intentionally or inadvertently.

In particular, I would like to thank Peter Gallie, Glennis and Kathy of John Taylor High School; Phil Collier of Walton on Trent Primary School and Don Noakes (EWO) for their help in various ways. And my wife for her patience with my pre-occupation and tolerance of the noise of my wordprocessor.

Thanks are due to HMSO, Derbyshire C.C. and The School Journey Association for permission to use copyright material. I alone am responsible for any errors that have occurred.

Neil Adams

1 How the law works

The old tag has it that ignorance of the law is no excuse. Perhaps a better statement would be that those who have to deal with matters relating to legal obligations must be able to show that they have taken all reasonable steps to understand and implement the law as it stands. That is necessary in a civilised and well-ordered society but it is often a difficult task.

It is difficult because the law is complicated, technical, changing, unpredictable and bureaucratic. Often it is unfair, though undoubtedly the law-makers of the time believed it to be just in accordance with the ideas of their day. When Rumpole, that crusty and loveable old hack of a barrister created by John Mortimer, observes to a client:

> 'Justice! What has the law to do with justice, old dear?'

his cynicism has a ring of truth about it.

Before the 1980s schools were relatively untroubled by legal issues and problems. The massive Education Act of 1944, much of which is still in force, largely governed the workings of the education system from the DFE down to the smallest primary school. The major changes which did occur such as the raising of the school-leaving age, the introduction of CSE and the development of comprehensive schools were largely accepted by society – the only issues being usually of a local and particular nature. No major Act of Parliament affecting schools was passed between 1944 and 1980.

Since 1980 there have been five Acts which have concerned schools closely, the implications of which will be considered in detail in the next chapter. The overall effects of these have been to focus media attention on schools and colleges, to encourage the interest and involvement of parents, to delegate wide powers to governing bodies, to create conditions of service for teachers and to increase dramatically problems of management and accountability for heads and senior staff. The interpretation and implementation of the new law lies increasingly with the schools themselves, rather than with LEAs, as staff and governors struggle to manage. The increasing awareness of parents of their rights to go to law over such matters as negligence has created additional worries.

All this means that a basic understanding of how the legal system works is essential if schools are to approach legal issues over management with awareness and confidence.

Where does law come from?

Many of our fundamental concepts in law are based upon customs recognised from medieval times, hence one meaning of 'common law' – that common to the realm. In theory, customs may still be recognised as legally binding but this is very rare. In practice, today law is created mainly by enacted legislation – Acts of Parliament and Statutory Instruments – and to some extent by case law.

Acts of Parliament

Readers will be only too familiar with these. They come about as a result of the policy of a particular government, often because such a change was promised in an election manifesto; because of public interest or pressure; because of some social, political or industrial pressure or simply in the hope of winning votes in the next election.

Two examples affecting schools will illustrate what happens. The Conservative government in office was committed to delegating powers to schools and their governing bodies as well as increasing the involvement of parents and extending their rights. An underlying motive was probably a desire to weaken the powers of certain authorities of the far Left in the process. Acting upon the *Taylor Report* a tentative move towards this was made in the Education Act of 1980. As Government confidence grew, the Education (No. 2) Act of 1986 was passed, creating many of the wide-ranging powers that governors have today.

The so-called 'industrial' action by teachers and their associations over salaries in the mid-eighties, which led to schools being closed and pupils being sent home or being taught on a part-time basis, presented the Government with a crisis. The public was becoming increasingly concerned. Teachers' contracts were so vague that interminable arguments ensued over what they could or could not be required to do. A government which had triumphed over troubles created by other workers and their unions was determined to defeat the teachers by legislation imposing conditions of service and this led to the passing of the Teachers' Pay and Conditions Act of 1987. In effect this enables the Secretary of State to determine teachers' salaries and the main terms of their contracts.

An Act of Parliament in draft form, known as a Bill while proceeding through Parliament, should not be taken literally. It has to go through both Houses, where changes may occur. The House of Lords cannot affect the passing of money Bills but it may cause others to be delayed for a considerable time unless changes are made. For example, in its 1980 Bill the Government wished to give parents the right to withdraw their children from sex education. The House of Lords would not agree and the Government gave in. If school governors decide sex education is to be given in a school then it is compulsory, providing it has due regard to morals and family life. As part of its policy a governing body might choose to allow parents the right of withdrawal. When a Bill has passed through both Houses and received the Royal Assent then it becomes an Act and thus legally binding. Unless specifically stated, an Act or a Statutory Instrument created under an Act is never retrospective.

Statutory instruments

Obviously, an Act itself cannot deal with the detail of much of the law that it contains and cannot cope with all eventualities that may arise as a result of the new law. Therefore an Act will often delegate power to a particular body or person to create subordinate legislation. To be legally binding this will usually be in the form of a Statutory Instrument (SI).

The powers given in this way must be within the terms of the Act but are often wide-ranging. For example, under the 1988 Act the Secretary of State has virtual power to make any changes in the National Curriculum, its subjects, stages and testing that he sees fit. There are safeguards against the misuse of such powers but they are far from satisfactory.

In theory, all such instruments are subject to Parliamentary control. They may be vetted by individual MPs or by a committee of scrutiny but so many are in transit that unless a particular concern is aroused most will go through the process of approval with little being said. They are also subject to challenge in the courts. Any aggrieved person may approach a judge of the Queen's Bench Division of the High Court claiming that the body or person concerned is acting *ultra vires*, i.e. beyond the powers granted under the Act. If the court is satisfied that the power granted by Parliament has indeed been exceeded then, by means of what is known as a prerogative order, the offender may be instructed to desist. To refuse to do so would constitute contempt. To approach the Queen's Bench in this way needs considerable determination and good legal advice.

The same court, by means of a similar order, may compel a body or individual to carry out obligations imposed upon them by Parliament – for example forcing an LEA to provide sufficient schools for an area.

DFE Circulars and Memoranda

These are included here because of the amount of material issued and the confusion that exists as to the nature of their influence. They are not a part of statute law and are not therefore binding upon LEAs and schools. Statutory Instruments are couched in legal language, frequently difficult to understand. The practice of the DFE is to issue Circulars and Memoranda endeavouring to explain their legal requirements and giving advice as to how those legal requirements may be met. The tone is often such that they read rather more like instructions than advice and are interpreted as such. Generally, however, the advice should be followed since, if difficulties arise between a school and LEA or between a school and parents, the advice can provide strong support for the action taken.

Of course, an LEA may take DFE advice and turn this into an instruction to a school which then has to be followed; but as schools gain more and more power to make their own decisions in many matters, they will be able to decide whether to follow the DFE line or not.

EXAMPLE

Education Reform Act 1988 S.4. – requires the Secretary of State to establish a National Curriculum (see figure 1).

SI 1990/1109 – details amendments to previous regulations concerning teaching provisions (see figure 2)

DFE Circular 7/91 – gives guidance on local school management (see figure 3).

Apart from the difficulties created by legal terminology and convoluted style, the problems of statute law are those of definition and omission. It is in these two areas that case law and the establishment of legal precedents provide remedies.

Case law

The working of an Act of Parliament or SI may not be clear. The terms may be so vague or general that they can be interpreted in various ways. It is in such situations that case law comes into play. A court will listen to the facts of a particular case which involves the interpretation of a term and will declare its meaning. In future, lower courts will be bound to follow that decision, courts of equal standing are expected to do so and higher courts, though not bound, will give it careful consideration.

Education Reform Act 1988

CHAPTER 40

ARRANGEMENT OF SECTIONS

PART I

SCHOOLS

CHAPTER I

THE CURRICULUM

Preliminary

Section

1. Duties with respect to the curriculum.

Principal provisions

2. The National Curriculum.
3. Foundation subjects and key stages.
4. Duty to establish the National Curriculum by order.
5. Courses leading to external qualifications.

Religious education

6. Collective worship.
7. Special provisions as to collective worship in county schools.
8. Religious education required in the basic curriculum: further provisions.
9. Exceptions, special arrangements and supplementary and consequential provisions.

Duties with respect to certain requirements

10. Duties with respect to certain requirements.

Standing advisory councils on religious education

11. Standing advisory councils on religious education.
12. Determination by advisory councils of the cases in which the requirement for Christian collective worship is not to apply.
13. Advisory councils: supplementary provisions.

Figure 1 The Education Reform Act 1988. Section 4 requires the Secretary of State to establish a National Curriculum.

STATUTORY INSTRUMENTS

1990 No. 1109

EDUCATION, ENGLAND AND WALES

The Education (School Curriculum and Related Information) (Amendment) Regulations 1990

Made - - - - 22nd May 1990
Laid before Parliament 22nd May 1990
Coming into force - 21st June 1990

In exercise of the powers conferred on the Secretary of State by sections 22, 103 and 232(5) of the Education Reform Act 1988(**a**), and after consulting with such persons with whom consultation appeared to him to be desirable, the Secretary of State for Education and Science hereby makes the following Regulations:

Citation and commencement

1. These Regulations may be cited as the Education (School Curriculum and Related Information) (Amendment) Regulations 1990 and shall come into force on 21st June 1990.

2.–(1) The Education (School Curriculum and Related Information) Regulations 1989(b) shall be amended in accordance with the provisions of this regulation.

(2) For paragraphs (1) and (2) of regulation 8 there shall be substituted the following paragraphs–

"(1) Subject to paragraph (2), the head teacher of every county, voluntary and maintained special school (other than a special school established in a hospital) shall make available to the governing body of the school not later than the relevant date such particulars of the educational provision which is intended to be made in the school in the relevant school year in respect of pupils in each year group as are referred to in paragraph (3).

(2) Where the educational provision intended to be made for one or more classes in a year group is substantially different from the intended provision for other classes in that year group paragraph (1) shall have effect as if the reference to each year group were a reference to each class of that year group.".

(3) For paragraph (3) of regulation 8 there shall be substituted the following paragraph–

"(3) The particulars referred to in paragraph (1) are:

(a) for a primary school:

(i) total lesson time per week, excluding time spent on registration;

(ii) the subjects or activities taught;

(**a**) 1988 c.40. For matters to be prescribed, see section 235(7) of this Act and section 114(1) of the Education Act 1944 (c.31), and for the transfer of functions to the Secretary of State see S.I. 1964/490, 1970/1536 and 1978/274.

(**b**) S.I. 1989/954, amended by S.I. 1989/1136.

Figure 2 Statutory Instrument 1990

Elizabeth House York Road London SE1 7PH

Circular No 7/91
22 April 1991

LOCAL MANAGEMENT OF SCHOOLS: FURTHER GUIDANCE

LIST OF CONTENTS

Figure 3 DFE circular

Obviously, the standing of the court which makes the decision is of great importance.

Teacher to pupil: 'Give me those cigarettes, Johnny Smith! You know cigarettes are banned in school. You're not having them back.'

The definition of theft in the Theft Act of 1968 is the dishonest taking of property belonging to another with the intention of permanently depriving the other of it. Assuming that the cigarettes are Johnny's property, they have been taken and there is a stated intention of keeping them. The only missing element is that of dishonesty. What constitutes dishonesty is not always easy to define but several cases have established guidelines for magistrates or juries in theft cases. A person is dishonest if he does something which ordinary reasonable people would consider dishonest and he is aware of that fact.

It is most unlikely that this teacher has been dishonest – the situation could have been dealt with easily anyway by informing the parents that the cigarettes were there to be collected. However, the writer once found a teacher smoking a cigarette from a packet confiscated from a pupil. That seems to meet the definition of theft.

Other cases have attempted to clarify the meaning of 'taking', 'property' and 'permanently depriving'. There is a steady stream of cases defining the meaning of the language of statute law.

A second function of case law is to declare the law where none seems to exist. The somewhat unrealistic theory is that the law does exist but it has never been declared publicly – the judge in the case is thus able to do so. This is very convenient. In order to reach a decision the court is in effect able to fill gaps in the law. There are a number of cases of significance for schools; the following is a good example.

Anne Ricketts and the bamboo bow and arrow

Ricketts v Erith Borough Council 1943

A boy in a Roman Catholic primary school brought a bamboo bow and arrow onto the school playground at lunch time. He fired the arrow, accidentally hitting Anne in the eye. The glass in her spectacles was shattered and considerable damage was done to her eye. One of the nuns was on duty and had visited the playground on several occasions but she was inside the building when the incident occurred. An action for damages was brought on grounds of negligence through inadequate supervision. The main argument was that a teacher should have been in the playground watching pupils continuously. If so, the accident might have been prevented. Earlier case law did suggest that teachers should take such care as good parents would – but nothing about pupils being watched continuously.

The judge dismissed the action but in doing so declared that such supervision on playgrounds should be reasonable and adequate in the light of the circumstances but it did not have to be continuous. The significance for schools is that on playgrounds and around school buildings patrolling staff is normally sufficient. The case does leave open what is reasonable and adequate in other particular circumstances.

There are three basic problems with case law. Which aspects of a case provide the elements which will bind subsequent hearings? Which earlier cases are relevant to the one under discussion? Which courts are bound by the decisions of which others?

Ratio decidendi

This is the reason for the judicial decision. Not all that is reported in the judgement on a case creates a rule to be followed by other courts – known as a binding precedent. Only the *ratio decidendi* does that. All other statements are known as *obiter dicta* (words by the way) and have persuasive influence only. What constitutes the *ratio decidendi* is not always clear and leads to further legal hair-splitting. We could perhaps say that the *ratio* of the Ricketts case is that supervision by teachers of pupils on playgrounds must be reasonable and adequate but not necessarily continuous.

Distinguishing

A court has to decide which earlier precedents are relevant to the case before it and which it may or must follow. Usually, it will be the function of counsel to bring these to the attention of the judge. He may 'distinguish' such precedents, i.e. declare them to be so different because of the circumstances that they do not apply in the present instance.

In *Blasdale v Coventry District Council 1981* pupils in a primary school were crowded into two separate classrooms during a wet lunch hour. A midday supervisor was on duty, moving from room to room. An eight-year-old child suffered an eye injury as a result of a paper clip flicked by another pupil – the supervisor being in the other room at the time. In this case the judge found that negligence was present because of inadequate supervision and thus, because of the special factors – very young child, indoors, crowded conditions, – distinguished it from the Ricketts case. It could be argued that this was a further clarification of 'reasonable and adequate' in supervision situations.

The courts

The importance of a case in creating a precedent and thus influencing later decisions depends upon its position in the hierarchy of courts, of which there are two kinds – **civil** and **criminal**. Criminal courts deal with all matters stated by statute to be criminal, or defined as such under the common law. Civil courts and tribunals deal with all others. The basic rule is that higher courts bind lower ones and that courts are expected, though not compelled, to follow those of equal standing. Clearly, one way in which to challenge an unpalatable ruling is to appeal to a higher court. This may follow the previous decision, overrule it or reverse it. Two examples which may have significance for schools will illustrate situations that exist.

1 Is detention a lawful punishment for a school to use?

The issue is important because unlawful restriction of a person's physical movement is a form of trespass to the person. To the best of the writer's knowledge there is only one case on record. This was heard in a Lancashire county court and the decision was that it was indeed lawful. No appeal was made and since county courts are the lowest in the civil hierarchy they do not create binding precedents. A later hearing in the High Court could easily declare detention to be unlawful.

2 May a governor who is a police officer take part in staffing appointments?

Mr Champion, a policeman and school governor in Gwent, was told by his Chief Constable that not only was he refused permission to have time off to sit in on appointments but he was forbidden to engage in such activities in his own free time. The main reason seemed to be that members of the public might then be given the impression that he might not act fairly in his capacity as a policeman though there also seemed an implication that he might know too much about candidates to be unbiased. There were visions of numerous crooks eager to join the teaching profession.

Mr Champion was angered by the ban and went to the courts. The case progressed through the system. At Court of Appeal stage the judges were in favour of the Chief Constable but, by majority, the judges of the House of Lords found for Mr Champion. So there the matter rests – police governors may sit in on staffing appointments but subject, of course, to rules of withdrawal affecting all governors. Only the House of Lords may change its own decisions and is always reluctant to do so. An Act of Parliament may change decisions made by any court.

The main advantages of case law are that it can provide certainty over many legal problems and yet give the courts scope and flexibility. Ironically, the disadvantages may be those of uncertainty in some situations and the encouragement of finicky and technical arguments.

Finding the law

Acts of Parliament, SIs, DFE Circulars and Memoranda are all obtainable from HMSO or booksellers. The DFE will send relevant material to LEAs and sometimes direct to schools. *The Law of Education*, published by Butterworths, consists of two large loose-leaf files, regularly updated. It contains all statute law relating to education and circulars and memoranda, plus details of many important cases. The original cost and that of updates is considerable, probably beyond the means of most schools. *The Head's Legal Guide*, published by Croner in loose-leaf form, does not reproduce the legislation but gives detailed comments on it and appropriate references.

Case law is more difficult. The reporting of court cases in newspapers and journals (except for *The Times* and one or two other quality dailies) is usually of little legal significance. Of these, reports in *The Times* are the most useful, widely respected and used by lawyers. The authoritative reports are to be found in the *All England Law Reports* and similar publications which may be available in main libraries. The major teacher associations will usually have details.

Criminal courts

Two of these may be of some concern to schools since they will deal with pupils or staff in trouble and for whom reports may be required.

Magistrates courts

These are the lowest in the criminal hierarchy (they have some civil jurisdiction over domestic matters and licensing also). They are staffed by a bench of lay magistrates though legally qualified stipendiaries sit in some large cities. The magistrates are assisted by a Clerk who is a qualified solicitor or barrister. A magistrate may sit alone but it is normal for three to preside, one acting as Chair. A single magistrate outside the court may issue warrants. Magistrates are also referred to as Justices of the Peace.

Normally, magistrates deal with all criminal matters in the first instance. Offences that come before them fall into three categories. Summary offences, e.g. speeding, can only be tried by magistrates. Serious indictable offences such as murder, rape or arson can be brought for trial only in the Crown Court, but the magistrates hold a preliminary hearing to decide if the evidence is strong enough for the case to go forward for full trial. Offences falling between the two categories are said to be triable either way – that is the offender is given the choice of trial by the magistrates or by a jury in the Crown Court. Theft by shoplifting is a good example. Where an accused chooses summary trial the magistrates reserve the right to pass the case on to the Crown Court for sentencing if a guilty verdict ensues.

Magistrates are limited to imposing a sentence of up to six months' imprisonment or a fine of up to £2000. The Crown Court's powers are limited only by the law relating to a particular crime e.g. ten years for theft. Other options open to magistrates include suspended sentences, probation and supervision orders, community service orders, conditional or absolute discharge or binding over.

Magistrates conduct separate hearings under special rules for those under 17. For criminal offences there are juvenile sittings for children and young persons – a child is anyone under 14 and a young person one over 14 but under 17. Prosecutions may not be brought under the criminal law against children under 10 – the age is eight in Scotland.

Appeals on criminal matters from magistrates' courts go to the Crown Court unless they are on a point of law, the process being known as 'case stated'. Such appeals go to the Queen's Bench Division of the High Court.

In domestic and civil matters magistrates sit in 'family proceedings courts'.

For juvenile and family sittings magistrates are drawn from special panels. Further discussion of the involvement of schools, pupils and parents in these proceedings will be found in later chapters.

Crown courts

These were created by the Courts Act of 1971 and replaced the old assizes and quarter sessions. They are strategically situated to cover the entire country. They have unlimited criminal jurisdiction, though some will be designated to deal with more serious crimes such as murder and others with lesser offences such as those triable either way.

When the Crown Court is hearing a criminal trial it consists of a judge and jury. The judge advises the jury and gives rulings on points of law that may arise but the jury decides on matters of fact and gives the verdict.

The sanctions available are limited only to those laid down for particular offences and may range from an absolute discharge to life imprisonment.

Appeals from the Crown Court go to the Court of Appeal (Criminal Division) or in special circumstances direct to the House of Lords, which is the final court of appeal on criminal matters. If the appeal is by way of 'case stated' on a point of law it goes first to the Queen's Bench.

Civil courts

These courts, together with tribunals, deal with all cases that are not covered by criminal courts. They have jurisdiction in family matters which may well affect schools and, as they deal with contracts, increasingly schools may become involved regarding the provision of goods and services.

County courts

These are the lowest courts in the civil hierarchy. Each court is a local one, the supposed purpose being to deal quickly and cheaply with a variety of minor legal cases of a civil nature. These include actions for breach of contract (e.g. unpaid bills); actions in tort (e.g. those for negligence, trespass or nuisance); undefended divorce cases; adoption and other family matters.

In many instances the decisions as to whether the case will be heard in a county court or in the High Court will depend upon the amount of money involved, though even where large sums are concerned a county court may deal with the matter if both parties agree.

The court is held by a judge or registrar – the former dealing with more difficult cases. The latter will deal also with cases in the small claims section where remedies are sought over relatively trivial matters, costs are minimal and parties usually appear in person, though solicitors do have right of audience here and in county courts themselves.

The main purpose in a civil action is for the court to hear the case of the plaintiff and defendant and decide between them on what is known as 'the balance of probabilities'. The burden of proof is lower than in a criminal court where an accused's guilt must be proved beyond a reasonable doubt and the only possible verdicts are *guilty* or *not guilty*. There is an additional choice in Scotland – that of *not proven*. A civil court, however, may decide that one party is at fault, that both parties are equally at fault, or that one is at fault to a greater degree and award damages accordingly.

The aim of damages is to compensate the injured party for the harm suffered as far as money can do so, though if the other party has behaved badly the damages may be increased as a form of punishment. Even where one party is in the right the damages awarded may be only nominal.

Other remedies are possible but only at the court's discretion. The main ones are injunctions which compel action or forbid it.

High Court

There are three Divisions – Queen's Bench, Chancery and Family. The last two should be of little concern for schools though a complicated domestic issue could reach this level.

Queen's Bench has both civil and criminal jurisdiction and several of its functions have been mentioned already in this chapter. Not only does it deal with contract cases involving large sums but it will also hear large claims for damages for negligence – perhaps as a result of a serious accident to a pupil at school.

Another function of Queen's Bench is to conduct what is known as 'judicial review'. This is the discretion to hear cases where the court is asked to deal with matters from inferior courts and tribunals where it is alleged that injustice or irregularity has taken place. By means of what are known as Prerogative Orders the court may take action to put things right. Thus a Prohibition may prevent a body or person acting *ultra vires* or beyond their legal powers, e.g. the Secretary of State taking upon himself powers over the National Curriculum which are not within his remit from Parliament. A *Mandamus* may order performance of a duty, e.g. commanding an LEA to provide school transport where it should do so by law.

Appeals from both county courts and the High Court go to the Court of Appeal (Civil Division) or, by special permission, direct to the House of Lords. This is the final court of appeal in civil matters.

Tribunals

Strictly speaking, these are not courts of law. They are legal hearings set up to deal with specific aspects, the aim being to take a deal of specialist work out of the overloaded court system. There are many of these so-called administrative tribunals, all created by Parliament with their powers defined and controlled by statutory authority. They include tribunals over income tax assessment, NHS services, public transport and so on. One is of the greatest importance. This is the industrial tribunal which deals with matters relating to employment law such as unfair dismissal or discrimination. The importance of this tribunal is emphasised by the fact that appeal from it goes to the Employment Appeal Tribunal which ranks as a division of the High Court and thus provides a clear path through to the House of Lords by way of appeal.

To all intents and purposes tribunals are conducted as if they were courts though with an emphasis on local hearings, informality and cheapness. Legal representation is not essential though anyone involved in an employment dispute would be wise to take legal advice. Tribunals consist of lay persons selected for their expertise in the particular specialist field. For major ones, such as industrial hearings, the Chair is a legally qualified person.

There are also what are known as **domestic tribunals**. These are bodies set up to deal with disciplinary problems concerning certain professions such as solicitors or doctors. No such tribunals exist for teachers.

Northern Ireland and Scotland

This book is concerned largely with the law as it applies to England and Wales. Northern Ireland (which, at the time of writing, still has direct rule from Westminster) has a similar legal system which operates in a comparable way. There are some differences – for example under the Fair Employment (Northern Ireland) Act of 1976 discrimination on grounds of religion or politics is illegal.

Scottish law is considerably different, having evolved over the centuries as a system in its own right. The structure of courts does bear some resemblance to the English system but there are important differences – for example there is no final appeal to the House of Lords on criminal matters. The decisions of English courts do not bind Scottish courts and vice versa though each may be strongly persuasive of the other. Undoubtedly, the Scottish decision over marital rape influenced a later English decision.

A common practice is for legislation affecting England and Wales to be succeeded by legislation covering the same ground but with variations. Much of the current legislation affecting education in Scotland is contained in the Education (Scotland) Act of 1980.

An up-to-date book on the law in Scotland is *General Principles of Scottish Law* by E.A. Marshall, published by Green/Sweet and Maxwell – 1991.

European Law

The United Kingdom joined the European Community in 1973. Since that time European Law has had an increasing effect on the law of this country – for example the House of Lords is no longer the final court of appeal in all matters. If a case involving a point covered by European Law reaches the House of Lords then it must be referred to the European Court of Justice for a decision. The lower British courts may refer matters covered by European Law to the European Court at any time for a preliminary ruling.At first European Law was concerned almost entirely with economic matters. As the Community has developed its influence has been felt increasingly in other areas such as those of employment, social welfare and the environment. To date, there is no effect on schools but, at the time of writing, ideas have been put forward which, if adopted, could affect the curriculum and other aspects.

The European Court of Justice should not be confused with the European Court of Human Rights. In 1950 Britain was a signatory to the European Convention on Human Rights and in 1966 accepted the competence of its Commission. There is an agreement to guarantee certain rights to all citizens, including the right to physical freedom, freedom of conscience, religion and family life. Education is one of those rights.

A citizen of any of the nations involved may bring a case to the European Court of Human Rights alleging a breach of one of the rights and ask for a judgement. Readers may well remember the action of two Scottish ladies (Ms Campbell and Ms Cosans) over the use of the tawse in a Scottish school as an instrument of punishment. Their appeal to the Court of Human Rights for corporal punishment to be banned was rejected but the Court declared that parents should be able to opt out of such punishment on behalf of their children if they wished. The Government tried to bring a suitable measure through Parliament allowing such choice but the notion of discriminating between pupils who could be struck and those who could not was so manifestly absurd that it failed. The only solution was a complete ban on corporal punishment in state schools and this came into effect on August 5th 1987.

Undoubtedly, *Campbell and Cosans* had a considerable effect on the subsequent change in the law.

Corporal punishment is still lawful in independent schools except where pupils are grant aided.

Further reading

A straightforward introduction is given in *The English Legal System* by K Eddey (1987), published by Sweet and Maxwell. Readers interested in full details could refer to *The English Legal System* by Walker and Walker (1985), from the same publisher.

2 The new schools

It is the mid-1970s and Mr Christian is the newly-appointed head of the Pilgrim High School. This has been created under comprehensive reorganisation by the amalgamation of a grammar school with two secondary modern schools. Mr Christian has the difficult task of forming a new school serving the local community and all pupils within a closely defined catchment area. There is immense potential here but a number of obstacles.

The LEA is bureaucratic and has many regulations which have to be identified and followed. Mr Christian has charge of a complex of buildings on split sites but his views on their re-structuring and re-furbishing are treated with scant respect by an autocratic county architect. He has no direct control over major building works and he cannot authorise minor repairs costing more than £100.

His newly-appointed governing body, though well-meaning, is of limited practical help since the governors know little of comprehensive schools and, in some cases, little of state schools. It consists mainly of members of the local squirearchy and local councillors awarded governship as recognition of long service and good conduct by the political group in power on the county council. These governors expect in the main that their duties will be confined to attendance at termly meetings, sitting in on staff appointments and putting in occasional appearances at school functions. Usually, they will back the head's requests for staffing, finance, facilities and equipment but they have no power to provide. Their approaches to the LEA usually hit the same wall of cotton wool as those of the head.

The school is staffed according to the LEA's formula. Mr Christian has inherited teachers of varying quality from the three schools. There are some ex-grammar school staff who do not see pastoral care as in any way their responsibility and ex-secondary modern school staff whose personal academic standards are poor and who accept very low standards of work from pupils. He had identified some promising young teachers from all three schools but is unable to give many of them responsible posts because of the limited number of incentive allowances available and the number of protected posts that exist. His efforts to put the right people in the right slots have led to confrontations between the LEA and the teacher associations. A few staff are incompetent, rebellious or overtly uncooperative. The contracts under which his teachers work are so vague that Mr Christian is unsure as to what he may or may not demand of them. Attempts at taking disciplinary action meet with prevarication from the LEA. Unless problem staff make sexual advances to pupils or steal pocket money there is little he can do but hope that they will move on (unlikely) or apply for early retirement (more certain). The salaries of staff are fixed and there are few ways of rewarding dedicated and highly competent teachers – they are the ones who are likely to move. Staff have no representation on the governing body and thus no right to be involved when major decisions are taken.

The parents are largely bewildered by what has happened – they had not been involved in the running of the original schools. They are not represented on the new governing body. They have no right to information regarding the school's organisation and activities, no right to reports on a pupil's work and progress, no right to consult staff, no right to know the school's examination results, no right to help for pupils with special learning difficulties. There are no rights where a pupil is disciplined. If a pupil is excluded or expelled there is only a right for the LEA to provide some sort of education in some other way. In spite of the 1944 Act's statement that '. . . pupils must be educated in accordance with the wishes of their parents' there is little scope for choice of school.

As far as a pupil is concerned there is a right to receive '. . ., an efficient full-time education suitable to his age, ability and aptitude,' but there is no consensus as to what that means. In effect, Mr Christian and his staff decide what the curriculum of the school shall be. If they are wise, considerate of the needs of all pupils, define aims and objectives and devise syllabuses and methods to meet those aims and objectives then pupils will be well served. If their thinking is dominated by cranks or extremists then the curriculum will be inappropriate, biased, perhaps really harmful for the future lives of many children. At least there is scope for initiative and professional judgment and expertise.

If we switch to the early '90s we find that Mr Christian is still in post, though nearing retirement. His job over the years has seen great changes through a spate of legislation, introduced by successive governments showing an unprecedented interest in education and spurred on by close attention from the media to the working of schools. Mr Christian may have negotiated the Slough of Despond and escaped from the Castle of Despair but he has not reached some kind of Heaven. The changes have brought heavy responsibilities, new problems of relationships, a climate of accountability and a complex array of difficulties to be overcome.

The changes brought about during Mr Christian's headship may be seen by summarising the main implications of successive major Acts of Parliament.

Education Act 1980

- Each school must have a governing body.
- That body must include elected parents and teachers.
- Parental choice of school is extended.
- LEAs must create committees of appeal over such choice.
- Information relating to schools must be available to parents.

Education Act 1981

- Defines special educational needs and provision.
- Allows LEAs to make assessment of such needs and make a statement regarding them.
- Entitles parents to appeal against such statements.
- Lays a duty on LEAs to provide help for statemented pupils.
- Lays a duty on schools to identify and provide help for pupils with less severe special educational needs.

Education (No.2) Act 1986

- Requires the making of new Instruments and Articles of Government for all schools.
- Gives wider representation on governing bodies to parents, teachers and other members of the community.
- Gives governing bodies powers over curriculum, staffing, discipline, exclusions, finance, premises and admission of pupils.
- Defines the powers of LEAs over such matters.
- Requires governing bodies to issue an annual report on their conduct of the school and hold an annual parents' meeting.
- Places restrictions on the handling of political issues and sex education in schools.
- Abolishes corporal punishment in state schools.
- Introduces the concept of appraisal.
- Requires LEAs to provide information and training for governors.

Teachers' Pay and Conditions Act 1987

This Act in effect gives the Secretary of State power to determine and control the salaries of teachers and their conditions of service. The power is exercised by means of a Statutory Instrument known each year as the Teachers' Pay and Conditions Act 1987 (Continuation) Order which creates an updated version of the School Teachers' Pay and Conditions Document – the so-called *Blue Book*.

Education Reform Act 1988

- Establishes the National Curriculum.
- Makes provisions regarding RE and collective worship.
- Establishes the National Curriculum Council, the Curriculum Council for Wales and the School Examinations and Assessment Council.
- Introduces arrangements for the local management of schools. This has the effect of increasing widely the powers of governors over finance, staffing and control of premises.
- Makes new provisions regarding admissions and numbers.
- Sets out the arrangements for the creation of grant-maintained schools.
- Makes provisions for charges in maintained schools.

By the time this book is published all secondary schools and most primary schools will already have been granted full delegated powers under the new legislation. Those who have not yet received them will do so in the very near future and so the remainder of this book is written under the assumption that all schools do possess those powers.

Mr Christian has now progressed to a situation where he has to work closely with a body of governors with whom he has a wide collective responsibility for the conduct of the school. In many ways he is in a more powerful position, yet he is more accountable. His governing body includes parents and teachers, LEA representatives, perhaps foundation governors or those from a minor Authority and those co-opted from the community outside. No one group holds overall power though that may still be possible by manipulation of appointment processes in some situations. Previously, the chair was almost always a political appointee – now it may well be a forceful person with long experience on the school's PTA. The governors have extensive responsibilities and powers which force them to take a close interest in the running of the school.

The LEA must allocate finance to the governors according to the number of pupils on roll and further sums under particular headings. It may retain control of expenditure under certain other headings, must see that a school's finance is subject to audit and may take over if things go radically wrong. The governors may authorise repairs and minor building projects subject to planning and building controls.

The governors have full powers over staffing. They decide, within their budget, how many staff they wish to employ and the number of incentive allowances and discretionary payments they wish to grant. They may decide on the level of Mr Christian's own salary. They decide on the appointments, discipline and dismissal of staff, both teaching and non-teaching, and need to set up a committee to deal with such matters. Providing that they act reasonably and within the law they may appoint and dismiss whom they wish.

The teaching staff work under conditions of service. The number of hours and days for which they may be required to work are laid down. Within those limits Mr Christian may ask them to carry out any duty which amounts to a reasonable instruction in their capacity as teachers or in relation to any special allowances which they receive. They have their own elected representatives – not delegates – on the governing body so that their views may be put forward. They have rights of appeal to the governors on staff disciplinary matters. They must take part in appraisal procedures.

Parents also have elected representatives – again, not delegates. They have rights to receive or discover a mine of information regarding the organisation and conduct of the school together with information relating to the performance and conduct of their own children. They may choose a particular school, providing that school has room. They may appeal to an independent panel if that choice is denied and on numerous other matters to the governors of the particular school their children attend. There is a right for pupils with special learning difficulties to receive extra help.

For pupils corporal punishment has been abolished. Mr Christian and his staff however are now in a more powerful position over school discipline. While the governing body may issue a general statement of policy over discipline and make any particular points, the head is responsible for setting and maintaining the standards of behaviour, including the making of school rules. Refusal by parents or pupils to comply may lead to the pupil's exclusion. The decision to take this action is in Mr Christian's hands alone, though there are complicated rights of appeal against such a sanction. Since there is now open enrolment, parents who do not approve of a school's disciplinary code may seek for a school place elsewhere.

Probably Mr Christian and his staff would have claimed previously that they were offering a curriculum suited to the needs of their pupils. Now the curriculum is largely determined by the legal requirements of the National Curriculum though, of course, those requirements are unable to determine exactly what happens in classrooms – that is still very much a matter of professional judgement by teachers. Not only does the law now require certain subjects to be taught; it also lays down minimum contents for those subjects, stipulates that testing of a defined nature shall take place at certain stages and that overall test results shall be public knowledge. There are some reservations. Pupils may be exempted under conditions from all or part of the National Curriculum; there is still a right for pupils to be withdrawn from religious education and corporate acts of worship; the governors may decide whether sex education shall be part of the curriculum and if they decide in favour of its inclusion then it must have due regard to morals and family life. If political views are involved in the curriculum then they must be presented in a balanced way.

All these factors mean a radical change in the system of schools that has operated with little change since 1944 – the one exception being the creation of comprehensive schools and the abolition of the 11+ examination. We need to examine the nature of the new establishments that have been created and the system that controls them.

Department for Education

Education in state-maintained schools in England and Wales is controlled by Parliament through the Department for Education. Northern Ireland has its own Department of Education and there is a Scottish Education Department though the latter plays a less significant part in the control of schools than its English counterpart.

Control of the DFE is in the hands of the Secretary of State for Education and Science. He has the duty of promoting education throughout the country and seeing that LEAs provide the sufficient schools and the efficient education that is required by the law. He may give directions to any governing body or LEA that he considers to be acting unreasonably and he may decide on issues between a school and its LEA or between LEAs themselves. He may require reports and returns from LEAs who may, in turn, require them of schools. His permission is required for a new school to be created or the status of a school changed. He is required to see that schools are inspected and this is done through Her Majesty's Inspectorate, either by themselves or under their direction. HMI are appointed by the Crown and not by the DFE.

Since 1944 the DFE has had wide powers and responsibilities but these have been so lacking in definition that LEAs and schools themselves have often been left to go their own ways. A good example is the requirement to provide an 'efficient education'. This was not defined and the few attempts by judges to do so in particular cases make sad reading for teachers. The increasing involvement of some LEAs in curriculum policy, the inability or unwillingness of some schools to devise a balanced curriculum and increasing public concern have all led to the creation of the National Curriculum and control from the centre. The growth of grant aided schools, directly controlled by the DFE, and delegated powers to other individual schools have increased the powers from the centre at the expense of the LEAs.

Local Education Authorities

The structure of local government consists of Councils elected to provide certain local services of which education is one of the most important. Until the introduction of the new legislation the influence of the LEA upon the schools in its area was direct and pervasive. The granting of degrees of autonomy to schools has seen that influence decrease to a great extent but an LEA retains a number of important responsibilities and residual powers:

- It must create an Education Committee and appoint a Chief Education Officer.
- It must see that there are sufficient schools for its area and that these provide suitably for the education of pupils according to their age, ability and aptitude.
- It is responsible for maintaining those schools and ensuring that school buildings comply with standards laid down by the DFE.
- It must enforce the education of all children between the ages of five and 16, either by full-time attendance at school or otherwise.
- Unless a school is grant-aided, the LEA must provide finance for a school and see that those funds are properly accounted for. In the event of mismanagement it may take over finance.
- It must state its policy over curriculum, see that the National Curriculum is implemented and that regulations relating to religious education and corporate worship are laid down. It must provide for the special educational needs of pupils who are 'statemented'. It has responsibilities relating to political views and sex education as part of the curriculum.
- It must provide a deal of information for parents, particularly over admissions policies. In this respect there must be consultation

with governing bodies and the creation of an independent appeals committee which may override both the LEA and governors.

- It must hear appeals from parents against the exclusion of pupils, though the last word is with the appeals committee just mentioned. Discipline is in the hands of the head and governors but if this has broken down the LEA may take over the conduct of schools under its control.
- It must see that each school has a governing body, though grouping under one body is possible. There must be an Instrument and Articles of Government for each and the LEA must appoint its own representatives. Free training must be provided for governors.
- Where pupils are entitled to free transport the LEA must see this is provided.
- Subject to complicated regulations an LEA may close a school, change the nature of a school or open a new one.

The schools

Schools today may be county maintained, voluntary controlled, voluntary aided, special agreement, grant aided, city technical colleges or independent.

County maintained

Here the LEA has responsibility for financing and maintaining the school though under delegated powers the governing body decides how funds shall be spent. The governors are responsible for running the school under the terms of their Instrument and Articles of Government. Together, these form the constitution of the governing body and must conform to S.3 of the Education (No.2) Act of 1986. This indicates the number and type of governors.

The number of governors depends on the number of pupils on roll. Thus, a school with up to 99 pupils has nine governors. Two are appointed by the LEA; two are elected by parents; one is elected by the teaching staff; three are co-opted and the head completes the group. The Instrument may replace one of the co-opted governors by a nominee from a parish or district council and the head may choose not to be a governor if he or she wishes. Schools with greater numbers on roll have a larger governing body. A school with 600 or more pupils has the maximum total of 19 governors – five LEA nominees, five parents, two teachers, six co-opted members and the head.

The governors decide on the number of staff to be employed, their appointment, discipline, dismissal and, within limits, any discretionary awards. Although the LEA is the employer and has a right to be consulted, it may only interfere if the governors have acted unreasonably or unfairly. As with other schools, the governors have a wide range of additional responsibilities.

Voluntary controlled

Schools in this category, usually of a religious foundation, are not owned by the LEA but are the property of trustees created in the past by a Deed of Trust. Their Instrument and Articles will differ in some respects from those of maintained schools but the LEA has full responsibility for their maintenance and finance and is the employer of staff. The special powers of governors, as compared to those of maintained schools, are limited to matters relating to religious education, acts of worship and the use of the school at weekends.

However, the composition of each governing body will be different. The total number will be the same but instead of co-opted governors there will be foundation governors appointed by the body responsible for the trust. Foundation governors must form at least one fifth of the governing body.

For most other purposes schools in this category function as if they were maintained schools.

Voluntary aided

Schools of this type have an origin similar to those of the controlled variety but have retained greater independence. The governors own the premises and are responsible for the external maintenance and building work, though they may receive aid of up to 85% of the cost. Running costs are met by the LEA. The governors are the employers of staff though salaries are paid by the LEA.

S.4 of the Education (No.2) Act lays down provisions for the governing bodies of these schools. There is no limit to the number of governors but those appointed by the foundation must always exceed others in number and one must be the parent of a registered pupil. According to the number of pupils on roll the LEA nominates governors and parents and teachers elect their representatives. The head is a governor unless he or she chooses otherwise.

The Instrument and Articles of Government for these schools are different from those mentioned previously and give greater powers to the governors, particularly over the admission of pupils, religious education and the use of premises.

Special agreement

There are only a very few schools in this category. Their position is very much the same as those which are voluntary aided except that the LEA are the employers and not the governors.

Grant maintained

This is a new type of school created by the Education Reform Act of 1988. In essence such schools are similar to those with delegated powers but instead of being under the control of LEAs they are under the direct control of the DFE. The process of 'opting out', as it is known, is a complicated one and involves two resolutions of a school's governing body and at least one secret postal ballot of parents, followed by an application to the Secretary of State. There is no guarantee that the application will be successful.

The Instrument and Articles of Government are made by the DFE but are broadly similar to those of other schools. The composition of the governing body is rather different. Where the school was previously of the county variety 'first' governors must be appointed and where the school was previously voluntary, 'foundation' governors are appointed and at least two of these must be parents of registered pupils. These governors must always outnumber the others. According to the size of each school there must be elected representatives of parents and teachers and the head is a governor *ex officio*.

The governors are the employers of staff and have powers of appointment, discipline and dismissal. They have full control of the premises even being able to buy and sell property. They may make contracts except where these might involve loans.

Schools that obtain grant maintained status receive an immediate benefit of a cash grant and, although they are subject to legislation affecting schools generally, have a considerable degree of autonomy. However, they do lose the benefit of services provided locally by an LEA.

The legislation concerning schools of this type is to be found in the 1988 Act from S.52 onwards. The DFE issues a booklet entitled *How to become a Grant Maintained School.*

City technology colleges

The 1988 Act under S.105 also introduced the possibility of the creation of these establishments. Although the DFE provides finance for their running the capital costs are shared with whoever wishes to found the institution, the aim being to interest industrial concerns.

These colleges must provide education for pupils of all abilities but with an emphasis on science and technology or the technology of the arts. They may only be set up in urban areas. They are in effect independent schools.

Independent schools

Although many of these schools are founded upon trusts they are basically commercial organisations. Under contracts parents pay fees in return for the educational services provided. (The Assisted Place scheme provides for payment of fees from public funds for a limited number of pupils at certain schools.)

Independent schools are not affected by recent legislation such as that concerning conditions of service for teachers, regulations relating to governing bodies or the National Curriculum. They make their own decisions in such matters. They are, however, open to inspection by HMI and may be closed if they do not meet certain criteria.

Special schools

These are schools which cater for pupils with severe handicaps, whether physical or otherwise. They do not form a separate category since they may fall into any of those mentioned above with the exception of grant maintained and city technology college. Their particular Instruments and Articles of Government or their Deed of Trust will reveal their status and constitution.

3 The new governors

The recent changes in the law have created a new breed of governors. Instead of token appointments and groups with illusory powers we now have governors elected by parties with a clear interest in the school concerned with some real control over finance, staffing and other matters. Those involved in school management in any way need to understand the structure, conduct, responsibilities, duties and powers of those responsible for their particular school. The test that follows should give you some idea of the state of your awareness.

Test yourself

1 How many members of your governing body are there and whom do they represent?

2 How often are meetings held? How much notice must be given? What is the quorum necessary for a meeting to be able to make formal decisions?

3 To what extent are the meetings and minutes of such meetings private and confidential?

4 Have your governors created committees? If so, which of these have full decision-making powers?

5 Have your governors made any decisions in relation to the curriculum?

6 What are the powers of your governors over the appointment, discipline and dismissal of staff?

7 Can they dictate over matters of pupil discipline?

8 What is the position of governors with regard to the exclusion of pupils?

9 What are the limitations, if any, on the power of governors to spend the money allocated to them?

10 What are the arrangements for fixing the admissions level for your school? How are governors involved?

Comments on these questions will be found at the end of this book.

If you are able to answer most of these questions with certainty then the rest of this chapter may only be of limited value for you. However, it is likely that you will only be able to give vague responses to many. The complete answers are to be found in a number of documents and a study of several of them in some detail is necessary for an understanding of the new governing bodies and how they function.

We have seen how the main provisions of the Education (No.2) Act of 1986 and the Reform Act of 1988 concern governing bodies. The first was largely responsible for creating the new groups and the second for giving them the delegated powers to manage, known as LMS. They were followed by the SI Education (School Government) Regulations 1989 and this completed the legal foundation for the working of the new governors. The main aspects dealt with are as follows.

Education (No.2) Act 1986

Creation of Instrument and Articles	Ss. 1–2
Composition of governing bodies	Ss. 3–4
Appointment of governors	Ss. 5–8
Grouping of schools	Ss. 9–10
The curriculum	Ss. 17–19
School terms	S. 21
Discipline	Ss. 22–28
Parents' Report and Meeting	Ss. 30–31
Political issues	S. 45
Sex education	S. 46
Corporal punishment	S. 47
Appraisal	S. 49
Information/training for governors	S. 57

Education Reform Act 1988

The curriculum	Ss. 1–5
Re/Collective worship	Ss. 6–13
Provision of information	S. 22
Admissions	Ss. 26–31
Financial delegation	Ss. 33–43
Staffing	Ss.44–46

Grant maintained schools	Ss. 55–104
Charges	Ss. 106–111

Education (School Government) Regulations 1989

Disqualification from membership	Ss. 4–7
Tenure	S. 8
Chair and vice-chair	S. 9 and S. 23
Meetings	Ss. 11–14
Publication of minutes	S. 24
Delegation of powers	S. 25
Committees	S. 26
Powers of the LEA	Ss. 30–31
Withdrawal from meetings	Schedule to the Instrument

Between them these three pieces of legislation provide most of the law relating to governing bodies though it must be remembered that elements of earlier legislation, from the 1944 Act onwards, may still be relevant. It should also be remembered that the DFE is constantly preparing and issuing Circulars and Memoranda which, although they may not have legal force, do explain the legislation and advise on its implementation.

These three documents have implications for the governing of schools on a national basis. There are two others which form the legal basis for the conduct of each school and which, by S. 1 of the Education (No. 2) Act (1986), must be created. These are the Instrument and Articles of Government. In the case of county and voluntary schools they are drawn up by the LEA; the DFE itself prepares them for grant maintained schools. The DFE also has Model Instruments and Articles but these do not have to be followed in every detail as long as the law is complied with. Thus, there will be minor differences from one authority to another. There will also be variations because of the differing status of each school – primary or secondary, county, voluntary controlled, voluntary aided or grant maintained. Therefore it must not be assumed that those applying to one school are the same as those applying to another. A close study of those for your own school is necessary.

Instrument

Typically, this will cover the following aspects:

Composition of the governing body
Position of the head
Appointment of parent governors
Co-option of governors
Terms of office
Meetings
Chair and vice-chair
Proceedings
Confidential items
Minutes
Position of the LEA
Correspondence
Availability of Instrument

Articles

These set out the duties, responsibilities and powers relating to the particular school. Typically, they will include:

Conduct of the school
General responsibilities
Governors and the LEA
Governors and the head
Curriculum
The head and the curriculum
Religious education
School terms
Discipline
Exclusions
Appeals
Finance
Annual report to parents
Annual parents' meeting
Admissions
Staffing
Appointment of head
Appointment/dismissal of staff
Premises
Health and safety
Availability of Articles

A close study of the Instrument and Articles for a particular school is essential since they form the legal basis for the conduct of that school. Unfortunately, it cannot be assumed that they are up-to-date. The rapid changes taking place in our system mean that the most recent developments may not be reflected in the two documents; LEAs are notoriously slow in bringing out revised versions, yet the changes in the law have to be applied.

For example, it may be a considerable time before all Instruments and Articles cover the changes brought about by LMS. Thus the important power of governors to delegate decision-taking powers to committees made possible under the SI Education (School Government) Regulations of 1989 is unlikely to appear. This SI indicates areas where powers may not be delegated but there are at least two where full powers may indeed be handed over. The governing body may delegate powers over staffing and exclusion of pupils to committees and such action will have significant implications for the management of any school.

The governor

A final point we need to consider is whether all these legal responsibilities and powers fall entirely upon governors as a group or whether some or all apply to individuals. The basic answer is that they apply to the governors as a legally constituted body and not to individuals. So no governor has personal responsibility. An individual governor may not make decisions or, say, give instructions to the head or staff, although we have just seen how a committee with delegated powers might do so. There are two exceptions with regard to powers.

With the previous consent of the governors the chair (or, in case of non-availability, the vice-chair) may make routine decisions in between meetings on behalf of the governors but must then report back at the next meeting. The legislation also allows the taking of a decision by a chair in an emergency when there is not enough time to call a special meeting.

The second exception is that of the head. Whether he or she has chosen to be a governor or not the head has powers to act over many matters but must then be able to account for those actions if necessary at a later date. These powers relate to many routine matters over finance, the curriculum, staffing and discipline. More serious is the power to suspend a member of staff or exclude a pupil. The head may do either without consultation but must then inform the governors and the employer – and parents in the case of exclusion – and be prepared to face the appeals that may well follow in either case.

Further reading

Heads and governors on appointment must be given a copy of the Instrument and Articles of Government relating to their school. All other employees must have access to them. It should therefore be easy to consult them. *The Law of Education* by G. Taylor and J. Saunders (1984), published in loose-leaf form by Butterworths, has all the Acts, SIs and DFE Circulars and Memoranda. Copies of individual items are available from HMSO.

Croner's Head's Legal Guide (1992) gives detailed comment and Croner also publishes the useful *The School Governor's Legal Guide* by C Lowe (1992).

4 Meetings

Storm over teacups

It was a wild winter's evening and the meeting of the governors of the Nonsuch School was poorly attended – only four and the head being present. The storm outside was reflected by the unrest within. First, Mr Cantankerous complained of inaccuracies in the minutes, all of a minor nature. He did this at most meetings and the clerk, Mrs Slapdash, responded angrily, accusing him of pursuing a personal vendetta against her. A heated exchange took place until the chair, Mr Havering, managed to restore order.

When it came to 'any other business' more trouble occurred. Without any previous warning Mr Wedgwood, a co-opted governor and owner of a local china shop, raised the matter of crockery. It had come to his notice by way of parents that on the last day of the previous term one of the staff, a Miss Overwrought, in a fit of temper had smashed a large quantity of cups and saucers, these being used for events such as parents' evenings and concerts. He moved a vote of censure on Miss Overwrought for her behaviour as a bad example for pupils. This was seconded by Mrs Wellright whose own daughter had run foul of the same teacher. The head gave a spirited defence of an otherwise excellent teacher and said that he believed she had offered to pay for replacements. All this was to no avail, the motion was carried and would thus appear in the minutes.

Mr Wedgwood then proposed that he supply replacement cups and saucers at a good discount. This was seconded but Mrs Wellright then accused Mr Wedgwood of profiteering at the school's expense (he shouted that he was only trying to do them a favour) and moved an amendment that he should provide a quote for consideration at a later meeting. This was not seconded but was carried with only Mr Wedgwood against.

As she was recording this decision Mrs Slapdash commented loudly that Mr Wedgwood should keep his business interests out of meetings. The enraged governor jumped to his feet, said that he withdrew his motion and swept out of the room, knocking over a tray of coffee cups as he did so.

The chair decided to leave the matter of replacement crockery in abeyance and closed the meeting.

To an outsider this may seem an unlikely tale concerning trivialities. Those closely involved in meetings know that only too often serious matters will cause little friction while minor matters and points of order do so. The writer remembers a governing body arguing for what seemed an interminable time over whether smoking should be allowed at its meetings. A skilled chair was needed to deal with the passionate feelings that were aroused and arrive at a conclusion that a 'coffee' break should occur at a fixed time during each meeting.

However, the story is not told in order to discuss the social psychology of meetings but to clarify a number of points concerning the meetings of governors; points which may have legal implications and will be of concern to heads and staff involved in them.

Complaints over the number of meetings held as part of the running of any school are legendary. Those that involve all staff, senior management teams, departments or any similar groups do not have a legal basis though terms of reference, an agenda and minutes are all desirable. Conditions could be set, of course. Meetings of the governors do have a legal basis – the Instrument and Articles – and must be conducted correctly if decisions are to stand.

Quorum

For any governors' meeting to pass binding decisions there must be a quorum. This will be defined in the Instrument. Usually, it will be three in number or one third of the membership rounded up to the next whole number. Are the governors of Nonsuch School quorate? Five are present but if the head has chosen not to be a governor then there are only four. If the total membership exceeds 14 then the meeting is not quorate. This does not mean that a meeting and discussion cannot take place. It does mean, however, that no binding decisions may be taken.

What happens if a meeting is quorate and one member leaves, thus losing the quorum? The meeting continues and takes decisions but if a query as to the quorum is raised then the chair declares the meeting not to have a quorum and it may only continue on an informal basis.

The Chair

The chair of any legally constituted group has powers of control. These include the power to rule on matters of order, decide who shall speak and for how long, decide on items to be confidential, to exclude persons from a meeting and adjourn the meeting itself. Of course, all these should be handled tactfully and objectively. The chair should see that the business is dealt with efficiently and decisions are reached wherever possible, yet give all a reasonable opportunity to contribute. Whether the chair has a casting vote or not should be clear from the Instrument.

The head and teacher governors may not chair governors' meetings or those committees with delegated powers.

Our Mr Havering has made some errors. He has allowed the clerk to become involved in argument and make comments. The clerk is not a governor. S/he may read the minutes or correspondence and supply information but not influence decision making. The discussion of Miss Overwrought's behaviour is out of place. If the matter is to go beyond the head it should have been dealt with by a committee of governors in case Miss Overwrought decides to appeal against a finding. If it was discussed the chair should have declared it to be confidential so that the record would not then be open to public scrutiny at a later date. Mr Wedgwood has a clear interest in the purchase of the crockery so his proposal should not have been allowed. If another governor had made the proposal then Mr Wedgwood should have withdrawn during the discussion. An amendment was accepted without a seconder – in fact, that is in order unless the Instrument requires otherwise.

Agenda

Each governor (and the head, if not a governor) has the right to request that an item be placed on the agenda if it relates in any way to the conduct of the school. There are no legal rules as to the nature of an agenda but practice usually has apologies first, followed by a consideration of the minutes of the previous meeting. This is useful since matters dealt with previously need to be confirmed on record and those remaining unsettled identified before further progress can be made.

The Nonsuch governors appear to have 'any other business' at the end of the agenda. This can create great difficulties, since it allows an individual governor to raise an issue which cannot be dealt with adequately without some research (Miss Overwrought's tantrum may be the figment of a pupil's imagination) or spring a surprise attack on the head or chair. Some Instruments require a period of notice to be given to the clerk for an item to be placed on the agenda and unless this is complied with there can be no discussion of it. Thus A.O.B. will not appear on the agenda. This requirement could probably be overridden by the wish of the meeting in a matter of urgency.

Minutes and resolutions

Mr Cantankerous was being difficult but the minutes must be accurate. This is particularly important since the advent of LMS as governors may now take many decisions without the consent or approval of the LEA and may be responsible if matters are mishandled.

A resolution must be proposed and seconded before it can be discussed. The chair decides whether an amendment is strictly that or is really in the nature of a separate proposal. Voting on amendments takes place first and then the substantive motion as altered. The method of voting is for the meeting to decide.

Confidentiality

The meetings of governors are private – even the Annual Meeting for Parents is not open to the public other than parents. The governors may resolve to allow others to attend any of their meetings but such persons may not vote. While individual governors should observe confidence over details of discussions at meetings there is no legal requirement for them to do so. Once the minutes have been approved they are a matter of public record anyway. The exception, of course, is that of any item declared to be confidential and this should be recorded separately. Any discussion of Miss Overwrought's behaviour would certainly come into this category.

Withdrawal

A governor with an 'interest' in a matter under consideration should take no part in a discussion or vote on it. The 'interest' will often be a pecuniary one, as it was in Mr Wedgwood's case – he had an obvious interest in a contract being formed. A teacher serving as a governor cannot take part in a discussion of his or her salary or possible promotion and neither may a parent where the discussion relates to the admission or discipline of his or her children. The governors may allow them to remain without participating but withdrawal is preferable.

Committees

Any group with wide-ranging responsibilities will need to form sub-groups to deal with specific topics or areas. Until the advent of LMS it was rare for governors to do this but their new duties have made it necessary for them to do so. The setting up and working of committees has always been a feature of school management – probably excessively so, since decision-making may then be unreasonably delayed or even avoided. The final decisions of such groups were always subject to the approval of the head or at least a senior management group. If the head had delegated power to make a final decision then he or she would have to take final responsibility, though legal implications would be rare.

Governors are now in the position where they have full responsibility for many final decisions relating to the conduct of their school and which are required by law. Most of these decisions have to be taken by the governing body itself. S. 25 of the SI Education (School Government) Regulations 1989 gives a full list of matters where powers may *not* be delegated. There are 21 of these. Some refer to matters likely to occur only once, if at all. An example is a decision to endeavour to change the nature of the school. Some will concern the governors at intervals – admissions policy or dates of school terms and holidays. Others will concern the curriculum – over sex education, religion, political issues and the National Curriculum itself. When there is a proposal to delegate powers to a committee a check must be made against this list.

Of course, committees may be set up to deal with any matters mentioned in the list but they must report back to the full governing body for a final decision to be made. The legality of the constitution, proceedings and decisions of such groups cannot be challenged though that may be so with regard to the final decision of the governing body itself.

The head has a right to be present at the meeting of any committee, whether it has delegated powers or not, unless it is concerned with his or her conduct or salary.

For any matter not included in the list in the SI full decision-making powers may be delegated to a committee. For the two areas already mentioned, those of staffing and the exclusion of pupils, there is express authorisation in S25.(3) and (4) of the SI. In these two areas the creation of committees to conduct first hearings is essential since both staff and the parents of excluded pupils have rights of appeal which must be heard by a second committee or the full governing body, less those members involved in the first hearing.

A committee having full delegated powers may be one which meets on a regular basis, a standing committee which meets as required or an ad hoc committee. The last named is the least satisfactory since it takes time to set up and there is a danger of urgency allowing some flaw in procedure to occur which will have significance later in an appeal. The second method will be most suitable for schools, certainly in the case of exclusions, that is a properly constituted committee which can be called to a meeting at very short notice.

Such a committee will need to be constituted according to the terms of the Instrument of Government for the particular school (as indeed may those without full delegated powers). Here is a checklist of items that should be included as a minimum:

Checklist for committees

1. Title
2. Objects and areas to be covered
3. Composition
4. Quorum
5. Notice of meetings
6. Chair and vice-chair
7. Head's right of attendance
8. Attendance of non-members
9. Agenda
10. Voting
11. Minutes
12. Confidentiality
13. Appeals

Individuals

Earlier it was stated that the individual governor has no power alone – power is in the hands of the governing body itself – except for the chair and the head (whether a governor or not). The SI of 1989 also makes it clear that while power to dismiss staff may be delegated to a committee it may not be given to an individual, so the head may suspend but not dismiss a member of staff. A similar rule applies over exclusions. Only the head may exclude and only a committee may consider matters after that.

Unless delegation is barred by legislation then power could be passed to an individual to make decisions. It is difficult to think of many situations that might qualify but one obvious one is the delegated power to a head to appoint – but not dismiss – certain staff.

Further reading

The Law of Meetings by Shaw and Smith (1979), published by Macdonald and Evans, covers the legal points. *How to run Committees and Meetings* by Michael Locke (1980), published by Macmillan, is more readable and gives useful practical advice.

5 Contracts

Before the changes in status brought about by the legislation of the 1980s maintained and aided schools had little concern for the law as it relates to contracts, though they would have been involved to a limited extent in matters affecting the employment of teachers. Whatever contracts existed were made by the LEA who chose contractors and the terms to be agreed. If there was a breach then the LEA had to deal with it. Schools had little say in such matters – often being in the position where they knew that they could obtain goods or services under better conditions but were powerless to do so. Now, schools with grant maintained status make their own contracts and schools with delegated powers, while not strictly parties to the contract, have considerable control over the spending of their money and may negotiate with outside contractors.

This means that it is necessary for school managers to understand the basics of the law of contract so that in negotiating, concluding an agreement and dealing with problems that arise they may act with confidence and avoid pitfalls. The contracts they will be concerned with include business contracts, contracts of insurance and employment contracts. Employment contracts are so important that they will be dealt with in a separate chapter.

What is a contract?

A contract is a legally binding agreement made between two or more parties. Business, insurance and employment contracts are presumed to be legally binding unless it can be proved otherwise. So-called 'domestic agreements' between relatives and friends are presumed not to be legally binding unless there is evidence to the contrary.

Once it has been established that a legally binding agreement exists then each party may sue or be sued for damages for breach of contract in the civil courts. In certain special cases – not contracts of employment – a court decree may even enforce performance of a contract.

Form

The popular idea of a contract is that of a written document couched in legal jargon and containing a number of clauses, many in small print. In fact, only a few contracts have to be in writing. Contracts involving consumer credit arrangements are an example. Contracts for the sale of land or of guarantee have to be evidenced in writing, which in practice amounts to the same thing. Most other contracts may be made by word of mouth. For example, handing over a sum of money to a shopkeeper in return for a bar of chocolate has all the elements necessary to form a binding contract but it is not in writing. Obviously, in many contracts it is advisable to use writing for the sake of clarity and to avoid misunderstanding.

What then are those elements necessary to constitute a legally binding agreement? They may be summarised as:

1 Offer

2 Acceptance

3 Legal object

4 Intention to create a legal relationship

5 Capacity

6 Genuine consent

7 Consideration

Offer and acceptance

Both must be clear, unequivocal and communicated to the other party. The offer must indicate what is involved in the contract and the acceptance must be in accord with the terms as stated. Any reservation or qualification prevents the acceptance from being legally binding. Thus an offer of a teaching post which is subject to LEA approval is not an offer in a contractual sense. A contractor who agrees to carry out repairs to school equipment for a certain sum but subject to his inspection of the work involved has given no acceptance.

School A

This is a school maintained by an LEA who are the employers. The offer of a teaching post by the interviewing governors is not binding since it is conditional on LEA approval. Since the offer is not yet in being neither is any acceptance by a teacher. The binding offer comes when the teacher receives it from the LEA. The acceptance is complete when the teacher posts it or delivers it. This position may well change as the powers delegated to schools widen.

School B

This is an aided school where the governors are the employers. Here the offer of employment is binding and so is the acceptance by the teacher. Neither needs to be in writing though it is advisable to record them in this way. Of course, if the teacher had obtained the post by making a false statement relating to qualifications or some other important factor, the contract would be void or could be made so by the governors.

With regard to offer and acceptance the following points need to be remembered:

1 Both offer and acceptance need to be definite and communicated.

2 Advertisements in shops or catalogues are not offers but merely 'invitations to treat'. The purchaser in ordering makes the offer which the vendor may accept or reject. The vendor may, of course, be liable under legislation such as the Sale of Goods Act or the Trade Descriptions Act.

3 Inviting a tender does not constitute an offer. The party tendering makes the offer which may then be accepted or rejected.

4 Acceptance may take place by conduct. A school leaves a message on an answer phone in an emergency asking a joiner to repair a broken window. He does so without a formal reply. The school queries the amount charged. A binding contract exists but only a reasonable sum would have to be paid – if necessary, a court would decide what was reasonable. If, however, the message had requested an estimate for the repair it would not have been an offer and the joiner could not accept by conduct.

5 An offer may be revoked at any time before acceptance but the revocation must be communicated.

6 An offer will lapse after a stipulated time. Otherwise it lapses after what is a reasonable time in the circumstances.

7 There are special rules regarding the use of post. An offer posted comes into force when it reaches the other party. An acceptance is complete as soon as it is posted.

Terms

Written contracts are often lengthy because there is a desire to spell out the conditions that are involved. What is or is not included can be the subject of much disagreement. The terms of a contract fall into two categories:

Express Such terms are clearly stated. *Comfy Carpets Ltd. offer to supply carpet of a particular quality, colour and pattern for the staffroom at a cost of £1000. This is to include underlay and fitting.*

Implied Here the terms are not stated because both parties knew, or ought to have realised, that they were included when the contract was made. There are implied terms that Comfy Carpets will lay and fit the carpet in a professional manner and that their bill will be paid. Disagreement as to whether a term is implied or not is decided if necessary by a court. In the following chapter, which deals with contracts of employment, we shall discuss terms that may be implied in a teacher's contract.

3 Legal object

For any contract to be binding the intent of the parties must be lawful. It may seem obvious that an agreement to commit a crime is unlawful, indeed it is likely that it would amount to the offence of conspiracy. However, it needs to be remembered that legislation such as the Health and Safety at Work Act is part of criminal legislation. A contract between a school and a contractor designed to subvert such legislation would be unlawful. The contract would be invalid and prosecution could follow. Contracts which are likely to promote corruption or offend against public morality – whatever that is – are also unlawful as are those in restraint of trade or employment.

4 Legal relationship

For any contract to have legal consequences the courts must be satisfied that a legal relationship exists between the parties. There is a presumption that agreements of a business nature create this and so a contract to supply goods or services to a school does not have to state that it is intended to be legally binding. If there is an intention that such an agreement shall not be legally binding then that must be stated clearly. There is a legal relationship between schools which charge fees and the parents who pay them and also between travel firms and schools which book holidays with them.

Other agreements, say between relatives, are known as 'domestic agreements' and do not usually create a legal relationship unless this is expressly stated.

A growing practice is for schools to raise funds by parents agreeing to contribute on a single or regular basis. It would be tactless, and probably unprofitable, to describe these to parents as legally binding agreements as a test case would probably find them to be domestic agreements. They might also lack the necessary ingredient of 'consideration' (see below).

5 Capacity

Unless they are so drunk or mentally impaired that they are unaware of what is happening all adults may make contracts and be bound by them. This is not so for minors. They may only be bound by contracts of employment and for what are known as 'necessaries'. These are goods which are actually required by a minor at a particular time and the supplier must know that they were necessary and has actually supplied them. Essential food and clothing would qualify but a hi-fi system would not – though no doubt the minor would not agree.

6 Genuine consent

There must be a real understanding between the parties – the consensus – and consent must have been given freely by each. Thus mistake over the identity of a party or of the very nature of the transaction, the making of a serious misrepresentation or the presence of duress may invalidate the genuineness of the consent given. However, since the principle of *caveat emptor* (let the buyer beware) applies in contract, lack of consent cannot be pleaded if one party has failed to read the terms of an agreement or made insufficient effort to understand their implications.

7 Consideration

In law of contract 'consideration' is a technical term and means something of value given, or given up, by each party to the agreement. Unless this is present no contract exists, though it is possible to make a one-sided agreement legal by recording it under seal in the form of a deed. Mostly, the consideration is obvious – a teacher gives his or her services in return for the salary paid by the employer.

There are a few points to note:

1. The law enforces promises and not bargains. While the consideration must be real it does not have to be adequate. A school which knowingly agrees to a contract for repairs at an exorbitant rate has no redress; neither does a parent who knowingly sends his child to a school with highly inflated fees. *Caveat emptor* applies again.
2. The consideration must not have been given in the past. A parent makes an unsolicited gift of a computer to a school. Weeks later he asks for a small token payment to be made which he can use for tax purposes in relation to his business. If such a payment is made no contract exists since the parent's consideration was given before an agreement was made. However, if a supplier made regular deliveries to a school tuck shop it could be presumed that consideration was promised on each occasion and the school would be bound to pay for goods received until the arrangement was terminated.
3. The performance of a duty cannot constitute consideration. A teacher who promises to give extra help to a pupil in normal school hours in return for a payment by parents is not giving consideration since it is his duty to teach effectively anyway. If he coaches outside school then the position is different and there is consideration on both sides.
4. Consideration may lie in the giving up of something of value. A school's neighbour has a right of way across a playing field. If he agrees to forego that right in return for a payment by the school then there is consideration on both sides.

Termination and remedies

A contract may be terminated by performance by both sides, by both agreeing to bring it to an end, by frustration, by the occurrence of a previously specified event or by breach.

Frustration means some situation that makes performance impossible, e.g. the long-term illness or death of a teacher or the closure of a school. A good example of termination by a specific event is the case of a teacher employed to cover for another on maternity leave. When the absent teacher returns the substitute's contract ends, whether this is a matter of weeks or months. Breach of contract only terminates if it is a breach of a condition – something that is of vital importance in the agreement – and even then the injured party may choose to let the contract stand and sue for damages. Breach of a minor matter – a warranty – cannot terminate a contract but allows an action for damages. A court may need to decide whether a breach is of a condition or a warranty.

The basic remedy for breach of contract is an action for damages in a civil court. Here the aim is, as far as possible, to compensate the injured party for the financial loss suffered. If a court believes that the losing party has behaved very badly then it may increase the amount of damages as a form of punishment.

Insurance contracts

These deserve a special mention since over the years schools have become increasingly involved with them concerning school visits, personal accidents to staff and pupils and liability to others. They are in a special class known as contracts *uberrimae fidei* (of the utmost good faith). The normal requirements of a contract apply to them, with the addition that all known relevant facts must be revealed by the party asking to be insured. Failure to do so may render the contract void. This is because the one party is in a good position to know facts which the other would be unable to discover with reasonable ease. Factors likely to concern schools would be physical handicaps or medical conditions, dangerous activities to be engaged in or convictions for driving offences if a minibus or staff car is to be used.

Contract for a school visit

Figures 4 and 5 show details of a contract for a school visit, reproduced by kind permission of the School Journey Association. The booking form and conditions are largely typical of such arrangements. Party leaders and heads would do well to study such documents carefully so that they are aware of their position if difficulties arise. This one is written in relatively plain English, others can be much more difficult to understand.

We can make a number of points:

1 All the ingredients for a legally binding contract appear to be present. However, the details and the accompanying brochure are not an offer. The offer is made by the client when the signed booking form is forwarded. The Association's acceptance completes the agreement and it is stipulated that the agreement shall be in writing. The Association may refuse any booking without even giving a reason.

Booking Conditions

1. Bookings are made with the School, Journey Association and are restricted to members of the Association. Membership costs £5 per school (+VAT) for five years. No booking will be accepted without a completed and signed booking form: by signing the form you agree to the conditions detailed here on behalf of all persons taking part in the tour. A contract exists once we have confirmed the booking' in writing.

2. ***Payments***
A deposit of £20 per person is required with the booking form; or £60 for tours including Eastern Europe/air travel/cruises and for courses; or £6 for SJA hotels or day excursions. If you book less than 7 weeks before the departure date, full payment is required with the booking. In all other cases an interim payment of £20 is required 10 weeks before departure; and the balance 7 weeks before departure. Travel documents will be dispatched on receipt of full payment. If final payment is not made by the due date the Association reserves the right to treat your booking as cancelled, and you may be liable for cancellation fees (see 4).

3. ***Free places***
Our voluntary services are given for schools. Our prices allow for one adult per10 pupils to travel free and it is expected in return that such adults will exercise proper control over the party.

4. ***If you cancel your booking***
When either individuals or the whole party are cancelled the following charges will apply:- (a) normally the deposit will be lost (b) if cancellation is advised less than 6 weeks before date of departure, 30% of the tour cost (c) if less than four weeks before departure, 45% of the tour cost (d) if less than two weeks before departure, 60% of the tour cost. Note: For Apex fare and certain other flights no substitutions can be made within four weeks of the departure date. However, in cases of serious illness or exceptional family difficulties, the Board of Management of the Association will consider some reduction sympathetically.

5. ***If you change your booking***
If you want to alter details of your booking we will do our best to help, but will make an alteration charge of £5 per person (maximum £100 per booking form.) If you change your tour date(s) within 6 weeks of departure, the cancellation charges in (4.) will apply.

6. ***If we change your booking***
In the unlikely event that we have to change your tour, we will inform you as quickly as reasonably possible. If we have to make a material change within seven weeks of departure and if you have made the final payment, you will be offered compensation:- (a) within seven weeks at £15 per person; (b) within two weeks at £30 per person. A material change is a change of port/airport in the UK (except between Heathrow and Gatwick or when coach transfer to the port/airport is included in the tour cost); or of resort/destination area; or hotel/hostel of different category; or if time of departure/return varies by more than 24 hours. Should you not wish to accept a material change and the cause is other than force majeure (see 8.) we will either provide an acceptable alternative tour or refund all monies paid plus compensation as detailed above.

7. ***If we cancel your booking***
The Association reserves the right to cancel your booking and in the event will return all monies paid to us or provide an acceptable alternative tour. A tour will not be cancelled after the date when full payment becomes due except for force majeure (8.) if you fail to complete your payments.

8. ***Force Majeure***
Compensation payments do not apply if any aspect of your tour is affected by matters over which we have no control including war, threat of war, riot, civil strife, terrorist activity, industrial dispute, government action Weather conditions, natural disaster, fire, traffic conditions, port regulations or technical problems affecting hotels / hostels / coaches / ships / trains / aircraft.

9. ***Travel delay***
Should delay occur to your sea/air/rail connection due to circumstances completely beyond our control we will endeavour to provide (a) light refreshments for delays from 3-5 hours (b) a main meal for delays over 5 hours (c) hotel accommodation for extended overnight delays.

10. ***Brochure descriptions***
Descriptions in our brochure are advertised by us in good faith and care is taken over accuracy. But while the Association does its best to secure accommodation and reservations requested, there is no guarantee that accommodation or rail/air/boat reservations will be available.

11. ***Our responsibility for your tour or visit***
The Association accepts full responsibility for the services offered in our brochures, leaflets and newsletters, including liability for actions or deficiencies of its employees agents and suppliers within the UK or overseas. We further accept responsibility for any negligence on the part of ourselves, or our suppliers (other than air or sea carriers, see12.) which might result in death bodily injury or illness of our client. We have taken all reasonable care to ensure that our suppliers are efficient and reputable concerns complying with local and national laws of the countries in which they operate.

12. ***Terms and' conditions of carriage***
(a) carriage by sea/air is subject to the carrier's own terms and conditions for carriage of passengers/property, which incorporate the provisions of the Athens Convention relating to the carriage of passengers and their luggage by sea1974. Our booking conditions and the carrier's are intended to supplement each other, but in the event of any inconsistency the Booking Conditions shall prevail. (b) Subject to (11.) above, carriage of passengers and their luggage by rail or coach is also subject to the conditions of carriage of the relevant carrier, which may limit the liability of the carrier to passengers.

13. ***Health***
At the time of printing no vaccinations are required for our tours, but as regulations may change you are advised to check with your school medical officer or the DHSS before travelling. You may wish to obtain leaflets SA40/SA41 from your local DHSS office or from us; these cover reciprocal medical arrangements with western European countries for visits to doctors / clinics /hospitals.

14. ***Insurance***
Once you have paid your deposit you are covered by the Association's insurance package. Cover within the tour price is underwritten by Municipal Mutual Insurance Ltd and includes protection of pupils, teachers IEAs and Governing Bodies. Cover is for:-

Medical expenses	Cancellation charges
personal accident	emergency service
personal luggage	departure delay
moneys	hazardous activities (if required)

and public liability to £5,000,000.
The policy carries an excess of £100 per person for each claim

15. ***Tour prices***
Prices shown in this brochure are based on the relevant exchange rates on 3.6.91, viz:-

France	10.08 Fr	Denmark	11.35 Kr
Spain	182.9 pts	Belgium	61.00 B Fr
Switzerland	2.5 Sw Fr	Greece	325 drmo
Holland	3.24 Fl	Italy	2185 lire
Poland	17000 zl	Germany	2.96 DM

Should currencies change in your favour, our prices will be modified accordingly.

16. ***Surcharges***
The price of a tour could be subject to surcharges on currency, aircraft fuel and scheduled air fares. Should this occur, the Association will absorb the equivalent of 2% of the tour price, excluding insurance premiums and amendment charges: only amounts in excess of 2% will be charged. Where a surcharge is payable there will be an administrative charge of 40p.
Should the surcharge amount to more than10% of the tour price, you would be entitled to cancel the tour with full refund of moneys paid, except for the insurance premium paid to us and any amendment charges provided that you cancel within 14 days from the date of the surcharge invoice.

17. ***Personal Injury unconnected with the tour package***
Should any member of your party, while on the booked tour/visit, suffer illness, personal injury or death through misadventure not connected with the tour arrangements or with any excursion sold through us, we shall offer you every assistance we can, including advice and initial financial assistance up to a limit of £5000 per booking. This service is underwritten by Municipal Mutual Insurance Ltd.

18. ***Complaints and Arbitration***
Any matter which may give rise to a complaint must be reported as soon as practicable to our representative or the hotel or supplier and/or the police, as appropriate. Should the complaint not be resolved immediately and you wish to pursue the matter, you must write to us within 28 days of your return. Disputes which cannot be settled amicably may be referred to Arbitration under a scheme administered independently by the Chartered Institute of Arbitrators by arrangement with the Association of British Travel Agents. The scheme provides for a simple and inexpensive method of arbitration on documents alone with restricted liability on the client in respect of costs. There is a limit of £7500 per booking form.

19. ***English Law***
Without prejudice to the rights of the client under section 16 the contract between the Association and the client shall be governed by English law and any dispute shall be determined by the English courts.

20. ***Definition***
In these Booking conditions:-
a) "The Association" means the School Journey Association and includes its employees agents and insurers.
b) "The client" means all persons named/listed by the person signing the Booking form.
c) "Suppliers" means all persons other than the Association, including employees, agents and subcontractors, who provide services or facilities which form part of the tour offered by the Association in this brochure.

The School Journey Association

Figure 4 Example of a contract

Booking Form

BOOKING FORM FOR TOUR TO ____________________

This form with £20/£60 deposit PER PERSON to be forwarded to the office or the Hon.Tour Secretary.

____________________ to whom all correspondence should be addressed

NO BOOKING ARRANGEMENTS WILL BE PROCEEDED WITH UNTIL THIS FORM WITH DEPOSIT IS RECEIVED.
PLEASE READ BOOKING CONDITIONS ON OPPOSITE PAGE.

NAME OF SCHOOL ____________________ PHONE NO __________

POSTAL ADDRESS ____________________

NAME OF DESIGNATED PARENT ____________________ PHONE NO __________

NAME OF PARTY LEADER ____________________ PHONE NO __________

and PRIVATE ADDRESS ____________________
between end of School Term
and Departure of Tour ____________________

DATE OF SCHOOL CLOSURE ____________________ DEPOSIT PAID __________

Has the fee for SCHOOL AFFILATION/MEMBERSHIP been paid to cover the current year? __________

When a school is affiliated all staff and pupils are eligible to participate in a tour without having to pay individual subscriptions.

REF NO OF TOUR REQUIRED __________ DATE & DAY OF DEPARTURE __________

DURATION __________ DAYS DATE OF ARRIVAL BACK IN UK __________

No of pupils		Boys	Girls	Total Pupils	Corrected totals (for office use)	Extra Meals
Age on date of departure	11 and under					Please state requirements for meals en route not provided in tour cost
	12-13					
	14					
	15					
	16-25					
	Total Pupils					
		Men	Women	Total Adults		
No of adults						
Please State if these totals include any married couples		Total of party				

Remarks (for office use only ____________________ SJA Reference No __________

____________________ Foreign Reference No __________

Optional Excursions

Excursions to	[illegible]	Price
1		
2		
3		
4		

State number of pupils who will be aged 16 years or over on the date of re-entry into United Kingdom __________

COUCHETTES State number required - if available

out __________ home __________

Couchettes are applied for 9 weeks prior to departure. **No refund can be granted** on couchettes cancelled within 4 weeks of departure.

I have read the booking conditions attached and accept them on behalf of the party and the parents

Signature of designated parent ____________________ Date __________

Signature of party leader ____________________

The School Journey Association

Figure 5 Example of a contract

2 Once the agreement has been made the client accepts all the express terms as printed.

3 In the event of non-payment by the due date the contract may be declared void. In the event of cancellation by the client there are penalties though these may be covered in whole or in part by the insurers. Therefore, parents should be told clearly that if there has to be cancellation their deposits might not be returnable.

4 Note the disclaimers on brochure description and force majeure.

5 The cover for an accident not occurring as part of the tour arrangements is a mere £5000 for each booking. This amounts to a gesture of goodwill rather than cover. A wider personal accident policy for individual pupils is worth considering.

6 There is a mention of 'hazardous activities'. This is somewhat vague. It would be wise for the client school to spell out to the Association particular dangerous activities to be included.

7 It may well be that there is an implied term in such contracts that staff will exercise proper supervision of the party. This particular contract makes that an express term. Failure to supervise pupils properly could be a breach of this contract.

A full discussion of school visits will be found later in this book when supervision and negligence are considered.

Further reading

Contract by F. R. Davies (1991), published by Sweet and Maxwell, is a concise and readable text.

Readers wishing to study contract in real detail are referred to the famous and complex Cheshire and Fifoot's *Law of Contract* (1991), published by Butterworths.

6 The contract of service

Until comparatively recent times a contract of employment was the same as any other contract. If it met the criteria explained in the last chapter than it was legally binding. The employer, usually being in the stronger position, could dictate terms which generally the employee had to accept. The union movement, the work of reformers and the changing attitudes of society and governments have all helped to bring about improved rights and protection for workers. Most of these rights are now enshrined in the Employment Protection (Consolidation) Act of 1978 with subsequent amendments and additions. Some common law provisions still apply. European Law is an influence that is likely to increase still further.

Those who work for others fall into two categories – employees (the old term was servant) and independent contractors. The latter is someone who does work for others and is paid by them but, to try to put it simply, is not under the control of the paymaster as to how and when the work shall be carried out. The independent contractor is self-employed. All other workers are employees and that includes teachers.

The distinction is an important one since the legal relationship between an employer and an independent contractor is based upon the ordinary law of contract and is known as a contract **FOR** services. That between an employer and employee is based upon the ordinary law of contract plus all the provisions of modern employment law. These create what is known as a contract **OF** service. The importance of the difference is well illustrated by the fact that an employer is rarely liable for the negligence of an independent contractor whereas he is liable for the negligence of employees who are acting within their course of employment.

Since teachers and others who are paid to work in schools are employees it is essential that those who manage schools understand the nature of a contract of service.

Formation

A contract of service is formed like any other contract with offer, acceptance and so on. It does not have to be in writing – that is a legal requirement for a few contracts only (those of apprenticeship being an example) but it is common for writing to be used. What is required under Section 1 of the 1978 Act is what are known as written particulars; these must be given to an employee within 13 weeks of taking up employment. The particulars include the job title, details of salary and method of payment, hours and conditions of work, holiday entitlement, sickness and injury benefits, pension rights, reference to discipline and grievance procedures and the notice to be given by either party. These are all terms of the contract.

Until the introduction of conditions of service for teachers full written particulars were not given to them – for example there was no agreement as to hours of work. Those particulars that did exist were contained in the *Burgundy Book: Conditions of Service for Schoolteachers in England and Wales*. This has now been supplemented by the *Blue Book: School Teachers' Pay and Conditions Document*, which is updated annually.

Terms

The basic principle of two parties agreeing to the terms of a contract by free negotiation is no longer generally true of a contract of service. Whilst it is possible for agreement to take place on many aspects, the requirements of employment law (see below) mean that certain statutory requirements must be met whether the parties like it or not. Most of these are for the protection of employees.

As with all contracts there are express and implied terms. Express terms will usually be found in written documents. For teachers these will include the letter of appointment, the written particulars mentioned above, the contents of the *Burgundy* and *Blue Books*, any regulations of the employer and a job description (if given) with details of the post. The statutory provisions are also express terms since only in very few instances may either party opt out of them.

Implied terms are more difficult since it is always possible for a court or tribunal to find that a new one exists. An example of this is to be found in a case concerning teachers, *Sim v Rotherham Metropolitan Borough Council, 1987*.

Cover

Before the introduction of conditions of service the express terms of a teacher's contract were few. Was attendance at parents' evenings or staff meetings outside school hours compulsory? Could staff be required to supervise before or after school? Could teachers be required to cover for absent colleagues? Heads did not know their position with regard to such matters, neither did members of staff nor the employers themselves.

During the mid-eighties the management of schools was seriously affected by strikes and so-called working to rule with teachers, on the instructions of their associations, refusing to carry out duties which were not express terms of their contracts but had usually been accepted as part of the job. Eventually, one such aspect reached the courts – that of teachers covering for the absence of colleagues. Miss Sim and other teachers, sponsored by the NUT, claimed that such cover was not a part of the contract and therefore voluntary. The employers claimed that it was a term.

The judgment, which went against Miss Sim, declared that, as with other professionals, the limits of a teacher's duties could not be defined precisely. A reasonable amount of covering for absent colleagues was indeed part of their agreement.

Faced with the prospect of public concern and a whole series of test cases on similar issues the Government was spurred into introducing conditions of service for teachers. This does not mean that further implied terms may not be at issue in the future.

Implied duties

It is well established that there are certain duties upon both parties which are implied. These are as follows:

An employer must:

- Pay salary as agreed
- Provide reasonable working conditions
- Observe provisions for sick pay
- Observe agreements as to hours of work and holidays
- Accept vicarious liability for employees
- Give time off for public duties
- Observe the statutory requirements of employment law

- Treat employees with trust and confidence

An employee must:

- Provide the services for which payment is made
- Carry out those services in a fitting and professional way
- Obey reasonable instructions
- Have regard for the employer's property
- Act in good faith towards the employer

Discipline

Before the growth of employment law the discipline of workers was a matter for employers; it usually meant dismissal. If the correct period of notice was given then the employee had no redress and the employer was not bound to give any explanation for the decision. If the correct period of notice was not given then there was a possible action for breach of contract, but this was a daunting prospect for all but a few employees.

Today it is normal for employers to give employees details of a system of disciplinary procedures. This is usually based on the Code of Practice drawn up by ACAS. There is no legal obligation on an employer to use this Code or indeed to have disciplinary procedures at all. However, when defending an action for unfair dismissal, it is useful for an employer to be able to show that fair treatment has included warnings as to misconduct and that efforts have been made to help the offender to put matters right.

Under LMS the responsibility for devising disciplinary procedures lies with a school's governors. They would be wise to adopt those agreed between the LEA and teacher associations.

The normal pattern is of a series of warnings of increasing severity:

Informal – the misconduct has been noted and unless there is improvement formal proceedings will be considered.

Formal – the warning is on a formal basis and may be given orally but is followed up in writing. It is now on record.

Final – this is a last chance situation and unless matters are put right dismissal will follow.

The procedures may commence at any stage. Where a matter is considered to be very serious a final warning might be issued immediately. In the case of gross misconduct, warnings could be dispensed with altogether and the offender dismissed. Procedures usually include rights of appeal against warnings and the right to have them removed from the service record after a period of satisfactory conduct. There is usually a right for a union representative to be present when warnings are given.

Vicarious liability

An important feature of the employer/employee relationship is the principle of **vicarious liability**. This makes an employer liable for the torts (civil wrongs such as negligence) of employees while acting in their course of employment. Apart from the fact that employers should take some responsibility for the actions of their workers they will also usually be in a better position to pay damages if any are awarded and should carry insurance for this purpose.

The liability is normally only for civil wrongs but it may be for some criminal matters under legislation such as Health and Safety. The injured party, say in a negligence action, may sue the employer or the employee or both jointly but it is the employer who will have to pay if damages are awarded. The employer may then sue the employee but this is unheard of since the employee is unlikely to be able to be in a position to pay. The usual course is for the employer to take disciplinary action instead.

It is important to remember that the employer is only vicariously liable if the employee is acting within the course of employment. This is not always easy to define but if the employee is carrying out activities approved, either explicitly or implicitly, by the employer or the activities are clearly connected with the employer's service then they will be within the course of employment. This applies even if the employee was acting in a negligent manner or was even disobeying instructions.

A teacher is told not to use pointed scissors with a class of very young children. She forgets the instruction, uses the scissors and a child is injured. The employer is liable though the teacher may be disciplined. The same teacher sends a very young child out of school on a personal errand for herself, without the permission of the head, and the child is injured. The employer is not liable – sending a pupil on personal errands for oneself is not within the course of a teacher's employment. What if the teacher had, with the head's permission, sent the young child to fetch something from a nearby shop to use in a lesson and an accident occurred? There is certainly negligence here (largely the head's) but the head is the agent of the employers and acts on their behalf. The teacher is within her course of employment since she has permission for her action. The employers would be liable – and angry. Heads can be disciplined too.

Termination

A contract of service may be brought to an end in any of the ways described in the last chapter, i.e. by performance, frustration, breach or notice. It is the consequences of the termination that often distinguishes it from other contracts.

A contract of service may come to end because of the death of the employee, long-term illness or injury which frustrates performance or the occurrence of a previously agreed event but it will usually be by notice.

Here the employee is in the stronger position. If he or she gives the correct amount of notice then the employer has no redress no matter what difficulties may be caused by the resignation – a teacher waits until the last possible day before resigning in order to create problems over appointing a successor. What if the employee leaves without giving the agreed period of notice? There is little that the employer can do except sue for damages for breach of contract – hardly worth-while – and the courts will not enforce the performance of a contract of service.

If the employer does not give the correct period of notice then the employee has an action for breach of contract or, more easily, an action for unfair dismissal. Even if the employer does give the correct notice then the employee may still claim compensation for unfair dismissal at a hearing of an industrial tribunal.

Unfair dismissal

Modern employment legislation requires that if a worker is dis-missed unfairly then the employer should pay compensation. Almost all workers are covered by this provision under Section 54 of the Employ-ment Protection (Consolidation) Act of 1978. Teachers and others who work in schools are included – the exceptions being those who have been in continuous employment for less than a year (two years in the case of redundancy) or five years if they work for more than five hours a week but less than 16. Fixed-term contracts may require an employee to waive rights over unfair dismissal and other employment benefits. The position over what constitutes continuous employment is often a complicated one and each particular situation needs to be checked carefully.

The dismissal may be clearly expressed or may be implied as **constructive dismissal**, a new concept deriving from Section 55 of the 1978 Act. With constructive dismissal the employer does not expressly dismiss, indeed the employee terminates the contract because of the unreasonable conduct of the employer which in effect amounts to a breach of contract. The basis is that the employer has made life so intolerable for the employee that resignation has been forced and thus the dismissal is an implied one. Even if the actions responsible are not carried out with the knowledge of the employer but by other employees then a claim may still be made, as in that of a female office worker who had been subjected to sexual harassment by male colleagues. Such a situation could easily be applied to some staffrooms.

Other possibilities in schools could be the removal of major responsibilities from a senior member of staff; a timetable for a teacher which was completely at odds with the terms of appointment; or some form of intimidation or bullying of a teacher by a senior colleague.

The basis of a claim for unfair dismissal is that, even though the correct period of notice may have been given, the employer has acted unfairly. First of all, the employee must prove that dismissal has taken place. Except in the case of constructive dismissal this is usually obvious enough. It is then for the employer to show that the dismissal was fair.

Dismissal on certain grounds is automatically unfair – because of membership or non-membership of a trade union or because ofpregnancy. Other reasons which will give the employer a strong case would include incompetence, dishonesty, misconduct, criminal conduct relevant to the contract and redundancy. Situations involving most of these factors will not always be straightforward. Unless the matter is obviously very serious from the outset then the employer will have to show that reasonable steps have been taken to make the employee aware of the complaints, that warnings have been given and help and advice have been afforded, e.g. that reasonable practical help has been given to a teacher having serious problems of discipline in the classroom. Redundancy, a new problem for schools, raises particular difficulties.

Redundancy

When the reason for a post ceases to exist there is no problem and the employee is entitled to certain benefits. Difficulties arise when there has to be selection for redundancy from a number of employees. A person may claim unfair dismissal if the redundancy procedures have not been handled fairly and already one or two schools have been in trouble because they have mishandled arrangements when selecting teachers for redundancy.

Let us suppose that a school, because of a falling roll and consequent loss of finance, has to lose several teachers. The following might constitute reasonable procedures to be followed:

1 The problem described to the staff as soon as possible
2 Volunteers for redundancy sought
3 Teacher associations consulted
4 Possibility of redeployment investigated
5 Objective criteria drawn up and published
6 Selection made strictly according to the criteria
7 Procedure for appeal against the decision

The most difficult element will be the drawing up of the criteria. Presumably, the first priority will be to ensure that the curriculum can be covered and this may mean an entire revision of the staffing structure. Other factors could include special responsibilities not connected with the curriculum or length of service at the school but, tempting though it might be, voluntary activities on behalf of the employee should not be included. If the employer has an agreed procedure for redundancies this should, of course, be followed.

Remedies

In Chapter 1 a brief account was given of the work of industrial tribunals. It is such tribunals that deal with complaints of unfair dismissal, along with other aspects of employment law mentioned below. When a tribunal accepts that a dismissal is unfair then the courses it may take are as follows:

Basic award

This is calculated in a way similar to that for redundancy and is related to age, length of service and rate of pay. It may be reduced if the employee has contributed to the dismissal by misconduct or has refused a reasonable offer of alternative employment.

Compensatory award

This is an award at the tribunal's discretion – if the employee has behaved badly there may be no award under this heading. The aim is to compensate the claimant for losses not covered by the basic award, e.g. for loss of pension rights or future earnings but there are no fortunes to be made under this heading.

Re-instatement/re-engagement

At the request of the complaint the tribunal may instruct the employer to give the job back (re-instatement) or find another post of similar status and salary (re-engagement). In either case there must be no loss of pension rights etc. If the employer refuses to re-instate or re-engage the tribunal has no powers of compulsion. Instead it may make a special award.

Special award

This is in the nature of a penalty imposed on the employer for not accepting the order of the tribunal and is also payable where the dismissal is related to union membership. It can amount to a substantial sum.

Employment law

The contract of service is subject to other areas of employment law in various ways. We can now make a list of most aspects likely to affect a contract of service at some time or other. Those marked with an * and only mentioned briefly so far will be included in comment on case studies used in the next three chapters:

- Legal requirements of a binding contract
- Express and implied terms
- Conditions of service*
- Salaries*
- Health and Safety*
- Leave of absence*

- Disciplinary procedures
- Discrimination*
- Dismissal
- Redundancy
- Unions*

Further reading

A good guide is *Employment Law* by Carr and Kay (1991), published by Pitman in the MacDonald and Evans (M and E) Handbook Series. There are many others.

Test yourself

1. When does a teacher's contract become legally binding on both parties?
2. What written information must be given to a teacher on or soon after appointment?
3. Where are conditions of service for teachers to be found? Are they definitive?
4. Miss Pretty, a PE teacher, has been offered a job with a popular dancing troupe, providing that she can start next week. She is under contract to the end of term but announces her intention of leaving on Friday. What is the school's position?
5. Rollasurface Ltd, whilst tarmacing a playground, cause an injury to a pupil. The pupil has been allowed by her teacher to go onto the playground while work was in progress. Who may be liable for any negligence?
6. What is meant by vicarious liability?
7. When is an employee working within the course of employment?
8. Are warnings essential as a part of staff disciplinary action? If so, what form should they take?
9. Employment protection means that although a teacher may be sacked compensation must be paid or re-instatement insisted upon by the tribunal. True of not?

10 Does an employer have full discretion over declaring certain employees redundant?

Comments will be found at the end of the book (page 199).

7 Managing staff – appointments, pay and conditions

The first five chapters of this book attempted to give you a basic understanding of the law and how it operates so that specific aspects of management problems might be approached more confidently. The previous chapter explained what is meant by a contract of service and gave detail of some of its more important aspects. We can now apply this to some particular problems, taking the opportunity to examine further aspects of the law of employment as it relates to schools.

Appointments

Probably the most important single factor in the management of schools is the appointing of staff since their quality and efficiency will be most significant in achieving success for the school and its pupils. Until the recent past the involvement of governors in appointments was real, though they were often content to go along with recommendations from the LEA or the head. Senior staff were rarely involved. Today, the governors, with certain reservations, have the power to appoint whom they wish, the influence of the head is likely to be even greater and the involvement of senior staff more common.

The Greyfriars School needed an English teacher. The following advertisement appeared:

> **THE GREYFRIARS SCHOOL**
>
> (11–18 comprehensive mixed. 1000 on roll)
>
> Required for September, a mainscale graduate teacher of English with subsidiary French to join a successful department. An interest in drama would be appreciated and 'A' level work possible for a suitable candidate. Full details available from the School on request.
>
> Applications by letter with a c.v. and names of two referees should be sent to the head at the School by 10th May.

Details supplied to would-be candidates included a description of the building and the area; a brief statement of the organisation and staffing structure; the approach to the curriculum and the work of the English department in particular; and a job description for the post. Amongst this information the following statements were to be found:

'*Teaching of English would be across the full ability range.*'

'*The department is all male so preference will be given to women candidates.*'

'*Candidates should indicate whether they have had any convictions for offences relevant to their possible employment as teachers.*'

'*Candidates called for interview will be paid reasonable expenses. Expenses will not be paid to a candidate who is offered the post but declines.*'

Applications were received from two men and a woman. The head and staffing committee of the governors, together with the head of English, decided to interview all three. Invitations were dispatched and letters of enquiry with details of the post sent to referees, time being short. References included the following statements:

'*While Miss Cherry is a very competent young teacher of both English and French, her active sex life outside school is a bad example for pupils*'

'*As far as I am aware, Mr Bunter's experience of French is limited to an O-level pass in the subject and participation in day trips to Calais in order to visit French hypermarkets.*'

The three candidates were interviewed by the head, the head of English and a governor, Mr Quelch. They were given a tour of the school in the morning and met other members of the department, with interviews taking place in the afternoon. The panel had prepared a list of questions but Mr Quelch suddenly added one of his own to the woman candidate: '*How do you think you would cope as the only woman in a large department?*'

All candidates were asked if they had read and understood the job description. Mr Bunter said that the description was somewhat vague as to the teaching of French and he was not prepared to teach this beyond Year 7 level. He could not offer drama but would be more than happy to help with the school's tuckshop. The third candidate, Mr Wharton, had some experience of school productions but made it clear that he only wished to be considered for the post if some A-level work could be promised.

The head of English was unhappy about all three candidates but he had no vote and the head and Mr Quelch eventually decided to offer the post to Miss Cherry. She accepted, though having private reservations as to the availability of night life in the area.

This incident raises a number of points.

Advertisements, details and job descriptions

Whether an advertisement constitutes a term of the contract is an open question as far as the law is concerned but the specific details of the post would certainly seem to be so. Schools should therefore be careful in the wording used, the accuracy of information given and any promises made or implied. For example, the successful applicant here is entitled to a proper share of English teaching, including that with abler pupils. Providing it is lawful, any condition may be made, so the refusal to pay expenses to an applicant who refuses appointment is permissible, though tactless.

Candidates may also make conditions; both Mr Bunter and Mr Wharton did so with regard to French and A-level work.

Job descriptions need to be approached with some care. Since the introduction of conditions of service a reference to the *Blue Book* virtually defines the job of a mainscale teacher. However grant-maintained schools may stray from this if they wish and independent schools decide their own conditions. It is necessary to give further details where allowances and extra responsibilities are involved. Here the description is part of the contract so when senior posts are being dealt with those additional responsibilities need to be clarified.

If it is desired to change a job description in a fundamental way after appointment, this can even amount to a termination of the contract and must only be done by consultation and the clear agreement of the teacher concerned.

Discrimination

The importance of avoiding discrimination in the making of appointments, in managing the day-to-day working conditions of staff and internal promotions has necessitated an increasing awareness on the part of school managers. The same awareness is needed in the treatment of pupils.

Discrimination legislation is based on two Acts of Parliament, the Sex Discrimination Act of 1975 (amended by the Act of 1986) and the Race Relations Act of 1976. These Acts do not only apply to employment. The legislation comes into force where a person is treated less favourably than others on grounds of sex, marital status, colour, race, nationality or ethnic origin. The discrimination may be direct or indirect.

Direct discrimination seems obvious enough, as in the incident of a head declaring that 'There were enough blacks on his staff already'. Indirect discrimination is more difficult. It may occur where an employer lays down a condition which means that by reason of sex or race etc. a person is treated less favourably, for example if it is stipulated that a number of years' teaching experience is required for a post – a condition which a married woman who had taken time off to have children could not possibly fulfil.

The employer may discriminate because of pre-conditions to employment, terms in the contract, lack of consideration for promotion, denial of training, victimisation and dismissal. The employer is also liable for discrimination practised by employees, for example racist remarks made to a coloured teacher by other members of staff, though the employer has the defence that it has taken reasonable steps to avoid this, e.g. by warnings or guidelines to staff.

Can discrimination ever be lawful? The answer is 'Yes'. It may be lawful (but not in Northern Ireland) on grounds of religion. Thus a school with a religious foundation may advertise for a teacher of a particular faith though, with certain exceptions, it may not advertise a post as being restricted to applicants of a particular sex. Two exceptions occur where there is a need to discriminate on grounds of decency or genuine occupational qualifications. Teachers who have to sleep in at a single-sex residential school may be included and so possibly may PE appointments in secondary schools. As far as race is concerned, a need for an employee to take on special duties with pupils from an ethnic group may apply, though a recent case decided that it was discrimination to bar consideration for such a post to a white candidate fluent in the particular language involved.

There can be problems of definition. In *Mandla v Dowell Lee (1983)* the parent of a pupil attending a private school insisted that the boy be allowed to wear a turban as required by his religion as a Sikh. The school refused to allow this since, as an independent school, it could enforce wearing of its own uniform. Were Sikhs a religious group or an ethnic group? If they were an ethnic group then there was unlawful discrimination but if only a religious group then the discrimination was not unlawful. The case went as far as the House of Lords which decided that Sikhs are an ethnic group so discrimination had taken place.

In the first place tribunals deal with cases of discrimination though on appeal they may go to the very top. The remedy is compensation. However, the tribunal may also declare the rights of the applicant and make recommendations to how the discrimination should be avoided.

We can find two instances of discrimination in the Greyfriars appointment (see page 63). To say that preference will be given to women candidates is discrimination against male applicants. To ask Miss Cherry how she would cope in working with an all-male department is discriminatory since the same question was not applied to male candidates. Both examples reflect recent cases.

Mr Mcateer applied for a post at an all-girls school in Northern Ireland where all the staff were women. Two men and five women were short-listed for two posts, one of which required special qualifications and experience in staff development. The tribunal accepted that on both aspects Mr Mcateer was superior to the woman appointed and that discrimination had occurred because he was a man. He was awarded £500 compensation.

In Haringey, Ms Makiya, at an interview for a post as inspector of technology, was asked how she would deal with reactionary male teachers in her specialism. The question was not put to other candidates. Although the tribunal considered she would not have been appointed anyway, the use of the question was held to be discriminatory and she was awarded compensation of £1750.

References

A person who gives references must do so in good faith. Whether the reference is shown to the person concerned is a matter for the two, though some employers have a rule that professional references for employees must be disclosed. Heads are obliged to give a reference for their teachers. What happens if the referee makes an error or creates a bad picture of a candidate for a post? Under the law of defamation – to be discussed later in this book – the injured party may sue for libel but the referee has the defence of qualified privilege which, in effect, means that the other has to prove malice.

If Miss Cherry could show that the statement regarding her was untrue and made maliciously then she has a possible cause of action though, having obtained the post, she has not suffered any damage. If she has kept her private life out of school then, in today's climate, that is her own affair. The comment regarding Mr Bunter suggests that his knowledge of French is very limited but he seems to have acknowledged this anyway at interview. If, in fact, he had taken French as a subject in his degree and the statement was made maliciously (there does seem a hint of this) he may have a cause of action.

Interviews

The interview is a vitally important stage of the appointments process. Not only does it offer a chance to assess candidates in person, it is also the point where a binding contract may be made, or at least an agreement which only needs ratification by an employer who has little choice but to give it. Based on what has been said here we can draw up a list of points to be remembered.

1. Draw up criteria for selection.
2. Check references for what may have been left unsaid.
3. Prepare questions beforehand.
4. Query any gaps in service record.
5. Ensure that statements do not conflict with details.
6. Ensure that candidates understand all important conditions.
7. Avoid questions that may be discriminatory.
8. Take a formal vote.
9. Make the offer clear and get a positive acceptance.
10. Record agreed reasons for the decision.

Rehabilitation of Offenders Act, 1974

Under this Act those who commit minor offences are entitled, after a prescribed time, not to reveal them when making employment applications. Exceptions are where the conviction is relevant to the post concerned. Teachers, like nurses or social workers, must reveal any convictions relating to those likely to come within their care; recent cases of child abuse have emphasised the need for this proviso and for careful checking. A teacher who has a previous conviction for a sexual offence, any other form of assault or theft must reveal it. If it is essential that the teacher drives a minibus and has a conviction for speeding then that should also be revealed. A person who has a conviction and reveals it may still be appointed.

The statement issued by the Greyfriars School regarding convictions is therefore a proper one though it would have been better to quote the Act and briefly summarise its provisions.

Conclusion

Greyfriars School needed to take more care over the details of the post it advertised, examination of applications and questioning at interview. As the influence of LEAs decreases in such matters schools will need to think carefully over appointments procedures, in particular over the gathering and checking of information regarding candidates. Increasingly, applicants are being asked to apply by letter rather than form. Here is a checklist of important data that needs to be obtained:

- Name and age
- DFE number
- Academic background – with dates
- Professional training – with dates
- Previous teaching posts – with dates
- Work experience outside teaching
- Further qualifications and courses attended
- Extra-curricular activities with pupils
- Interests outside school and relevant to the post

Conditions of service

Earlier we saw that teachers are now employed under a contract of service which has express terms contained in the *Blue* and *Burgundy Books* and possibly under other terms declared on appointment and accepted by the employee. Additional terms may be implied if a court is satisfied that they were understood by both parties to be present – remember Miss Sim and cover for absent colleagues.

Ginger Man

Mr Lancaster has just taken over as head of the Plantagenet School, a large primary school with a staff of 20. He is faced with the task of injecting some new life and enthusiasm into a school which had been allowed to coast along under a cosy routine by a head of long standing who has just retired. Mr Lancaster wants to ginger things up and perhaps make a name for himself in the process – at interview the governors had given him the impression that this was what they wanted, indeed expected.

A committee of governors had been set up to deal with staffing matters, including discipline. Mr Lancaster wanted to impress them and set about his task eagerly. He spent a week studying the organisation, routines and curriculum practice and then, at very short notice, called a full staff meeting which lasted for over an hour. The staff were shaken and irritated since previously such meetings had been rare. Many had to cancel outside commitments or had to make emergency arrangements for their young children to be looked after. They were even more shaken at what Mr Lancaster proposed.

There would be an immediate review of the staffing structure, incentive allowances and special responsibilities. Job descriptions did not seem to exist and so they would be drawn up. Teaching groups and methods would need to be re-examined. His inspection of records had shown an alarmingly high rate of absence among staff. There appeared to be a dearth of extra-curricular activities and he expected staff to contribute to these. He realised that staff involvement was important and so he would set up a pattern of groups to meet on a regular basis to deal with curriculum matters. Appraisal would be implemented as soon as possible. Once his reforms were complete the school should be a more efficient and dynamic institution which would attract more pupils and thus more finance to allow further expansion.

Some of the staff were particularly nervous. Mrs Mortimer had held a special allowance for some time with responsibility for environmental studies. She was an excellent teacher and was, in truth, given the allowance in order to retain her services. There was no stated policy over the environment in the curriculum. Mr Mowbray held office in one of the teacher associations and the previous head had allowed him a great deal of time off in order to attend meetings. Mrs Percy had very young children and, without considerable notice, could not stay for very long after school. She was often absent because of her children's illness and had made it clear that she could not be involved in out-of-school activities. Miss Douglas had an evening job as a barmaid and made sure that this enjoyable work was not affected by the demands of preparation and marking.

Posts and allowances

Mr Lancaster has every right to re-examine his staffing structure and make recommendations to his governors. However, he needs to remember that staff are employed under the express terms contained in the *Blue* and *Burgundy Books* and that any implied terms are arguable. Thus he cannot change the defined responsibilities of an allowance holder without being sure that this is permitted under the terms of appointment or the holder has given clear consent. A mathematics coordinator cannot be switched easily to look after special needs. Mr Lancaster may be lucky in that some allowances remain to be allocated or that there is some scope for additional ones. A careful study of his present structure and the provisions of Part III of the *Blue Book* will tell him what his position is.

He must check to see that both existing allowances and any proposed new ones comply with at least one of the criteria laid down in the *Blue Book*. These are that:

- the teacher is undertaking duties additional to those common to the majority of teachers;
- the teacher has shown outstanding ability in the classroom;
- the teacher is being employed to teach a subject where there is a shortage of teachers;
- the teacher is employed in a post which it is difficult to fill.

The allowance for Mrs Mortimer could be justified on grounds of her excellence as a teacher, but such a decision would be likely to offend other good teachers. It would be better to negotiate a new definite responsibility with her – she would probably be relieved – but Mr Lancaster cannot insist on this. He could demand that she take real responsibility for environmental studies.

Salaries

Once, salaries were linked to rigid scales set by the Burnham Committee. Employers could be generous or mean with extra allowances within clearly-defined limits but there was no further room for manoeuvre. Independent schools, of course, always had their own salary arrangements, some paying above Burnham and some well below. They are still free to negotiate their own terms with teachers.

Such freedom has not been allowed to state schools but there is now an increased discretion which may well have brought considerable management problems with it. Full details of the regulations applicable to both salaries and allowances are to be found in the *School Teachers' Pay and Conditions Document* – the *Blue Book* – plus explanatory circulars from the DFE. These are updated annually so reference to the latest edition is essential when dealing with related problems.

Governors are referred to as the 'relevant body' – before LMS it would have been the LEA. In both grant-maintained schools and schools under LMS the governors must have a policy over salaries which is available to staff and is kept under review. It is here that the first problem occurs.

Clearly, the governing body itself has to decide the policy but, since a member of staff with a grievance over pay has a right of appeal, there must be proper arrangements for that appeal to be heard. It would be improper for those hearing the appeal to have taken part in the making of the original decision, so it is necessary to set up a committee to deal with salary matters, the members of the committee not taking part in the hearing of an appeal. The same committee could deal with other staffing matters such as appointments, discipline and redundancy.

There is still a standard scale for teachers which is based on years of service but this may be supplemented in various ways. The most obvious is that of awarding the incentive allowances already mentioned. The number of these depends upon the group of a school; that, in turn, is based on its unit total. The allowances range from A–E and they are allocated within a range according to a group. The relevant body must award the minimum number of allowances available but the maximum is advisory and may be exceeded with justification.

A second way of supplementing salaries is by making appointments up to two points higher than is required on the standard scale. If Mr Lancaster's school is desperate for a music specialist but cannot find an incentive allowance then it could offer an appointment to a teacher on a point or two higher on the standard scale than that teacher was entitled to. A third way is by accelerating progression up the standard scale by one point at any time during the school year. A fourth is enhancing the payment at an incremental point within the sums allowed by the regulations, providing this is still below the next point on the standard scale, this arrangement being against stated criteria and subject to annual review. Either of the last two may be in addition to any incentive allowance payable. Finally, the relevant body has discretion to extend the top of the standard scale in recognition of excellent service, particularly in relation to classroom performance.

Teachers who work in special schools and those with special qualifications and whose teaching commitment in ordinary schools is largely of pupils who are blind or deaf must be paid the equivalent of an incentive allowance B on top of their entitlement on the standard scale.

Heads and deputies are paid on a single pay spine ranging over 51 points. The unit total is used to place a school within one of six groups – four in the case of special schools – and each group covers six normal positions on the spine. The relevant body places each head or deputy on the point that it sees fit, bearing in mind the particular difficulties and responsibilities involved; outstanding performance may also be considered. There is no incremental progression but the position is open to review. Any movement up the spine is not allowed for the immediate enhancement of pension benefits either for heads or deputies. The same rule applies to the salaries and allowances of other teachers.

The unit total which determines the group of a school is of fundamental importance in any of these calculations since it creates norms for the payment of heads and deputies and the number of incentive allowances. It is calculated thus:

Each pupil under 14	*2 points*
Each pupil aged 14 and under 15	*4 points*
Each pupil aged 15 and under 16	*5 points*
Each pupil aged 16 and under 17	*7 points*
Each pupil aged 17 and over	*9 points*

Numbers and ages are based on the return made on DFE Form 7 or its equivalent; age is taken to be that on the 31st August preceding the submission of the form. Pupils who attend for up to half a day only count half points. Pupils statemented for special educational needs count for three extra points each if in a special class and may do so anyway at the discretion of the relevant body.

It has not been possible here to give full details of salaries and allowances – for example we have not considered the position of reorganised or newly-opened schools, or payments to unqualified teachers. Neither have we given the current levels of salaries and allowances since they change from year to year. They can all be found in the latest edition of the *Blue Book*. What can be said is to emphasise once again that relevant bodies need to check carefully with the regulations before declaring a policy or deciding individual salaries or allowances that depart from the norm.

Professional duties

The express duties of a teacher under a contract of service are now contained in the *Blue Book* Part X, reproduced in full as Figure 6. Most of the tasks mentioned have always been recognised as part of a teacher's job but whether they could be insisted upon was open to question. There are now definite requirements that can be demanded of teachers but when words like 'reasonable' are used there are likely to be further arguments. There remains always the problem of what has been left unsaid.

The conditions make it clear that teachers may be required to:

- Teach
- Work up to a maximum number of 1265 hours
- Work for 190 days with pupils in school

PART X – Conditions of employment of school teachers

Exercise of general professional duties

33. A teacher who is not a head teacher shall carry out the professional duties of a school teacher as circumstances may require–

(1) if he is employed as a teacher in a school, under the reasonable direction of the head teacher of that school;

(2) if he is employed by an authority on terms under which he is not assigned to any one school, under the reasonable direction of that authority and of the head teacher of any school in which he may for the time being be required to work as a teacher.

Exercise of particular duties

34. (1) A teacher employed as a teacher (other than a head teacher) in a school shall perform, in accordance with any directions which may reasonably be given to him by the head teacher from time to time, such particular duties as may reasonably be assigned to him.

(2) A teacher employed by an authority on terms such as those described in paragraph 33(2) above shall perform, in accordance with any direction which may reasonably be given to him from time to time by the authority or by the head teacher of any school in which he may for the time being be required to work as a teacher, such particular duties as may reasonably be assigned to him.

Professional duties

35. The following duties shall be deemed to be included in the professional duties which a school teacher may be required to perform–

Teaching

(1) (a) planning and preparing courses and lessons;

(b) teaching, according to their educational needs, the pupils assigned to him, including the setting and marking of work to be carried out by the pupil in school and elsewhere;

(c) assessing, recording and reporting on the development, progress and attainment of pupils;

in each case having regard to the curriculum for the school.

Other activities

(2) (a) promoting the general progress and well-being of individual pupils and of any class or group of pupils assigned to him;

(b) providing guidance and advice to pupils on educational and social matters and on their further education and future careers, including information about sources of more expert advice on specific questions; making relevant records and reports;

(c) making records of and reports on the personal and social needs of pupils;

(d) communicating and consulting with the parents of pupils;

(e) communicating and co-operating with persons or bodies outside the school;

(f) participating in meetings arranged for any of the purposes described above;

Assessments and reports

(3) providing or contributing to oral and written assessments, reports and references relating to individual pupils and groups of pupils;

Appraisal

(4) participating in arrangements made in accordance with the education (school teacher appraisal) regulations 1991 for the appraisal of his performance and that of other teachers;

Review: Further training and development

(5) (a) reviewing from time to time his methods of teaching and programmes of work;

(b) participating in arrangements for his further training and professional development as a teacher;

Educational methods

(6) advising and co-operating with the head teacher and other teachers (or any one or more of them) on the preparation and development of course of study, teaching materials, teaching programmes, methods of teaching and assessment and pastoral arrangements;

Discipline, health and safety

(7) maintaining good order and discipline among the pupils and safeguarding their health and safety both when they are authorised to be on the school premises and when they are engaged in authorised school activities elsewhere;

Staff meetings

(8) participating in meetings at the school which relate to the curriculum for the school or the administration or organisation of the school, including pastoral arrangements;

Cover

(9) supervising and so far as practicable teaching any pupils whose teacher is not available to teach them:

provided that no teacher shall be required to provide such cover –

(a) after the teacher who is absent or otherwise not available has been so for three or more consecutive working days; or

(b) where the fact that the teacher would be absent or otherwise not available for a period exceeding three consecutive working days was known to the maintaining authority or, in the case of a grant-maintained school or a school which has a delegated budget and whose local management scheme delegates the relevant responsibility for the provision of supply teachers to the governing body, to the governing body for two or more working days before the absence commenced;

unless –

(i) he is a teacher employed wholly or mainly for the purpose of providing such cover ("a supply teacher"); or

(ii) the authority or the governing body (as the case may be) have exhausted all reasonable means of providing a supply teacher to provide cover without success; or

(iii) he is a full-time teacher at the school but has been assigned by the head teacher in the time-table to teach or carry out other specified duties (except cover) for less than 75 per cent of those hours in the week during which pupils are taught at the school;

Public examinations

(10) participating in arrangements for preparing pupils for public examinations and in assessing pupils for the purposes of such examinations; recording and reporting such assessments; and participating in arrangements for pupils' presentation for and supervision during such examinations;

Management

(11) (a) contributing to the selection for appointment and professional development of other teachers and non-teaching staff, including the induction and assessment of new and probationary teachers;

(b) co-ordinating or managing the work of other teachers;

(c) taking such part as may be required of him in the review, development and management of activities relating to the curriculum, organisation and pastoral functions of the school;

Administration

(12) (a) participating in administrative and organisational tasks related to such duties as are described above, including the management or supervision of persons providing support for the teachers in the school and the ordering and allocation of equipment and materials;

(b) attending assemblies, registering the attendance of pupils and supervising pupils, whether these duties are to be performed before, during or after school sessions.

Working time

36. (1) (a) a teacher employed full-time, other than in the circumstances described in sub-paragraph (c), shall be available for work for 195 days in any year, of which 190 days shall be days on which he may be required to teach pupils in addition to carrying out other duties; and those 195 days shall be specified by his employer or, if the employer so directs, by the head teacher;

(b) such a teacher shall be available to perform such duties at such times and such places as may be specified by the head teacher (or, where the teacher is not assigned to any one school, by his employer or the head teacher of any school in which he may for the time being be required to work as a teacher) for 1265 hours in any year, those hours to be allocated reasonably throughout those days in the year on which he is required to be available for work;

(c) sub-paragraphs (a) and (b) do not apply to such a teacher employed wholly or mainly to teach or perform other duties in relation to pupils in a residential establishment;

(d) time spent in travelling to or from the place of work shall not count against the 1265 hours referred to in sub-paragraph (b);

(e) such a teacher shall not be required under his contract as a teacher to undertake midday supervision, and shall be allowed a break of reasonable length either between school sessions or between the hours of 12 noon and 2.00pm;

(f) such a teacher shall, in addition to the requirements set out in sub-paragraphs (a) and (b) above, work such additional hours as may be needed to enable him to discharge effectively his professional duties, including, in particular, the marking of pupils' work, the writing of reports on pupils and the preparation of lessons, teaching material and teaching programmes. The amount of time required for this purpose beyond the 1265 hours referred to in sub-paragraph (b) and the times outside the 1265 specified hours at which duties shall be performed shall not be defined by the employer but shall depend upon the work needed to discharge the teacher's duties.

(2) In this paragraph, "year" means a period of 12 months commencing on 1st September unless the school's academic year begins in August in which case it means a period of 12 months commencing on 1st August.

Figure 6 Contract of service for teachers

- Work for up to five days without pupils being present
- Spend sufficient time outside school for preparation etc
- Take part in meetings
- Prepare reports, assessments and syllabuses
- Consult with parents
- Provide reasonable cover for absent colleagues
- Maintain pupil discipline
- Ensure the safety of pupils by supervision
- Undergo training and appraisal
- Attend assemblies
- Carry out any reasonable instruction of the head

Mr Lancaster is in a powerful position and may require performance of all these duties from the staff at the Plantagenet School. If, however, he fails to approach his teachers with tact and consideration he will find that the conditions of service could impose severe limitations on the developments that he has in mind. In the first place he has to consider management of *time*.

Time

We have seen that Mr Lancaster can require his staff to work for up to 1265 hours in a school year; this should take place during 190 days when pupils are in school and up to five days when they are not. The only other time requirement is that spent outside school preparing and marking work and writing reports, but that Mr Lancaster is unable to quantify. Any additional time spent by teachers is voluntary.

He must make sure that the absolute essentials are covered – the curriculum and supervision – and then see what is left for other important matters. His plan might look something like this:

Plantagenet School

Directed time for teaching staff

School day for pupils	9–12 : 1.30–3.30
School day for staff with pupils	8.50–12.05 : 12.55–3.45
School day for staff without pupils	9–12 : 1–4

Staff hours with pupils = 190 × 6.05 hrs.	= 1155 hrs 50 mins
Staff hours without pupils = 5 × 6 hrs.	= 30 hrs
Staff and group meetings	= 14 hrs
Parents' evenings	= 8 hrs
Additional supervision before school	= 8 hrs
Total available directed time	= 1265 hrs
Total directed time allocated	= 1215 hrs 50 mins
Time remaining for allocation	= 49 hrs 50 mins

Notes Dates and times of meetings and parents' evenings will be announced in the school calendar.

Time for additional supervision will be used for a rota of staff to supervise on patrol from 8.40 each day.

Hours remaining will be allocated by the head as and when required.

The merits of a scheme on these lines are that the classroom hours are covered and responsibility for supervision of pupils before and after each session is made a contractual requirement. Time is allocated for important meetings and consultation with parents and hours remain to increase any allocations which prove to be inadequate or to cope with unforeseen situations. There is a recognition of the common problem of pupils arriving before the stated time; while a school may inform parents that it will not accept responsibility it is wise to have a member of staff present a little early.

If Mr Lancaster is able to establish an atmosphere of trust and professional commitment then his staff are unlikely to worry unduly over the allocation of time. If, however, he does not handle things well he may have situations where staff are calculating the amount of time spent and challenging his arrangements. Inevitably, there will be individuals who will present problems, however well he handles things. He needs a plan for directed time and this needs to be communicated to staff, say in the staff handbook. If there are significant changes involved then he should seek the views of union representatives and the staff generally.

If Mr Lancaster adopts this scheme then he has covered the main sessions and coped with supervision before and after. He has not included the lunch period and staff cannot be required to supervise during this time or even remain on the premises. They can be required to supervise during morning or afternoon breaks.

Mr Lancaster's stated intention is to develop out-of-school activities. Can staff be directed to take these? The answer is probably 'yes', if the hours can be found within the allocation and they are at a reasonable time. But the limits of directed time make this unlikely and so they will have to be voluntary. He will arouse resentment and possible refusal if he tries to pretend otherwise. For example, if staff accompany pupils on a residential visit then, strictly speaking, they are on duty for 24 hours of the day and entitled to count this as directed time unless Mr Lancaster has made it clear that this is entirely voluntary. His recognition of their help would be valuable.

What of Mrs Percy, the lady who has young children and will not help with out-of-school activities? Mr Lancaster may find ways of helping her which do not antagonise other members of staff but, providing she has reasonable notice, he can require her to conform to his time plan before and after school and by attending meetings and parents' evenings. Her domestic arrangements are a matter for herself and not the school. She cannot be compelled to take part in any extra-curricular activities unless these are in directed time.

The conditions require teachers to spend enough time out of school to deal with preparation, making reports and marking books. Undoubtedly, this is a grey area since the position will vary from teacher to teacher. If there is a suggestion that a teacher is not preparing or marking work adequately, perhaps as a result of parental complaints, then Mr Lancaster or one of his senior staff will have to monitor performance, collect evidence and if necessary consider disciplinary proceedings. Miss Douglas, the barmaid, may have few other commitments and be able to get her marking and preparation done between school closing and bar opening times. If so, well and good – but she will need to take time off in order to attend parents' evenings or any other activity in directed time. If she does not mark or prepare her work properly then Mr Lancaster must take action.

Reasonable instructions

The second limitation on what Mr Lancaster may do is expressed in the conditions of service as that of reasonableness in his instructions and allocation of duties to his staff.

What is reasonable? Each issue will raise a particular problem and a decision as to reasonableness under a contract of service will be made by a tribunal or a court in the last resort.

Any instruction to carry out a task which is not a term of the contract is not only unreasonable, it is breach. If Mr Lancaster orders any of his staff to undertake any activity, including teaching itself, outside of directed time then he is acting unreasonably. He will have to depend on voluntary help for most out-of-school activities. If he instructs teachers to supervise during the lunch period then he is acting unreasonably.

To date there have been no cases, to the writer's knowledge, on reasonableness as stated in the *Blue Book* but no doubt they will come. Mr Lancaster has probably raised one possibility. He has called a long staff meeting without giving adequate notice and has caused problems for some staff. This seems unreasonable. The conditions of service require teachers to attend assemblies and there is a legal requirement for corporate acts of worship to be held in schools. Would it be unreasonable to force a professed atheist to attend an act of worship? The writer thinks so.

Instructions to carry out professional duties expressly stated or implied by the contract and within directed time will always be reasonable providing adequate notice is given. They will even be reasonable without notice if some crisis occurs or if pupils are at risk. Problems are likely to arise from dealing with matters in an arbitrary or insensitive fashion. Consultation, planning and tact should enable school managers to avoid most of them.

Absence

The third problem that Mr Lancaster has found is that of a high rate of absence amongst staff. This is bound to lead to disruption of pupils' education and progress and some dissatisfaction for other staff who have to cover for colleagues or help supply teachers to cope. The absence of a primary school teacher is even more disturbing than that of a member of a secondary school staff.

An abnormally high rate of absence is difficult to deal with since the reasons may be complex. Low morale, stress, lack of commitment, professional inadequacy, overbearing and insensitive management attitudes and the presence of unscrupulous or particularly vulnerable individuals may all be significant factors. Mr Lancaster will have to understand when his staff may be absent legitimately and then deal with his problems in various ways.

The main reason for absence will probably be sickness. Here statutory sick pay must be given and responsibility for this lies with the employer who, in the case of teachers in state schools, must follow the conditions laid down in S.9 of the *Burgundy Book* though there is discretion to enhance them. As part of the written particulars given on appointment teachers must be given details of the relevant scheme. The basic provisions are:

- in the first year of service full pay for 25 working days and, after four calendar months service, full pay for 50 working days;
- during the second year of service full pay for 50 working days and half pay for a further 50;
- during the third year of service full pay for 75 working days and half pay for a further 75;
- during the fourth and successive years of service full pay for 100 working days and half pay for a further 100;

These are entitlements during any period of one year.

Long-term illness may allow an employer to terminate a contract; if the illness creates a situation where it is impossible for an employee to provide services required under the contract then the agreement may be void on grounds of frustration.

The second legitimate reason is for maternity leave, the regulations for which are also to be found in S.9 of the *Burgundy Book* and which are again more generous than statutory provisions.

The regulations are again somewhat complicated and are based on continuous service. At least a year's full-time service, or the equivalent part-time, is required and staff paid at hourly or daily rates do not qualify. Time runs from immediately before the commencement of absence and this should not be before the eleventh week of the expected week of confinement. Pay is granted to those with less than two years' service on the understanding that the teacher will return to complete at least 13 weeks' service, or part-time equivalent, otherwise the maternity pay may have to be refunded. The right of absence is for 18 weeks. Other provisions include:

- After two years' service there is a right to six weeks' maternity pay, whether there is a return or not, and up to 29 weeks' post-natal absence.
- Notice of return must be given 21 days before the date by those with less than two years' service and seven days beforehand by those with two or more years' service.
- The date of return may be postponed by up to four weeks on production of a medical certificate.
- There is a right to time off with pay to visit an ante-natal clinic.

- Maternity leave counts for incremental purposes.

One question that arises is whether, on return from maternity leave, a teacher must be given an exact timetable and duties as carried out previously. The answer is likely to be that providing the new duties are within the terms of appointment and the conditions of service there is no right to exact replacement. Any fundamental change, however, would almost certainly amount to constructive dismissal and express dismissal on grounds of pregnancy is, of course, automatically unfair.

It will be noticed from the preceding explanation of sickness and maternity leave that the amount of continuous service that has been completed is of some importance. For full-time teachers, service moving from one employer to another counts. For part-time teachers working 16 hours a week or more this is normally also true; the part-time service counts proportionately towards full-time service. If a teacher works eight hours a week or more, but less than 16, then the part-time service may count if the teacher has been employed with the same employer for five years and under a single contract.

An employer must also give teachers reasonable time off to perform public duties such as serving as members of local authorities, sitting as magistrates, serving on tribunals or on school governing bodies. Pay is at the employer's discretion. Up to ten days a year may be given for service as examiners or moderators with examining boards and details are in the *Burgundy Book* Appendix 4. There is a right to reasonable time off for union purposes and this is usually regulated by local agreements between unions and employers. Employers must release employees for jury service but may appeal to the court for exemption – for example where a specialist teacher was preparing pupils for a forthcoming examination and the trial was likely to be a lengthy one. Teachers who have been declared redundant have a right to reasonable time off in order to seek other employment.

Other forms of absence, such as that on compassionate grounds, are at the discretion of the employer and may be with or without pay.

Unauthorised absence of any other kind is a breach of contract and a disciplinary matter unless this is strike action within the terms of current industrial legislation. Even so, the employer is entitled to withhold pay and continuous service may be affected.

We have seen that Mr Lancaster can compel Mrs Percy to carry out professional duties in directed time whatever domestic problems this might create for her. She may be absent because of her own sickness but is not entitled to be away because of the illness of her children. That could be covered by some compassionate leave. Her difficulties need to be handled with care. Cavalier treatment could encourage her to disguise her children's illness as her own and if this occurred only occasionally then proof would be difficult. If her absence amounts to a great deal then a medical report could be sought from her doctor and her dismissal sought but that is a last resort and could produce a claim for unfair dismissal. There may be other reasons for her absence and help might be possible.

Mr Mowbray is a different case. Mr Lancaster needs to check the agreement for union representatives and see that this is observed.

Heads and deputies

Before the introduction of recent legislation the exact role of the head was as ill-defined as that of an assistant teacher. A popular phrase was 'captain of the ship'. Perhaps the analogy was a good one – put in sole charge of a small isolated community, accountable to distant owners and with almost unlimited power over crew and passengers. Mutiny did occur from time to time, though most of the ships were happy ones. Apocryphal stories abound of heads who never left their offices; who refused to see parents or barred them from their school; who introduced rules which involved measuring the length of hair or a skirt with a ruler or devised punishments for pupils of carrying a rucksack filled with bricks on their backs or washing out their mouths with carbolic soap; who bullied or intimidated staff in various unpleasant ways.

Today the position is very different. If the head is still captain of the ship then the owners are near at hand, boarding parties are common, the crew know their rights and the passengers and their relatives are more vocal. There is a bewildering array of charts to be consulted.

All this does not mean that the head has become less powerful. Indeed, a head who is competent, balanced and sensitive and who is able to inspire trust and confidence is in an even more powerful position. The difference is that the head is now accountable to a governing body, to parents and pupils and the community generally and this is made clear in the duties defined in the *Blue Book* Part VIII.

These onerous duties are reproduced here in full as Figure 7. As with those for assistant teachers, many of them would have been understood by effective heads and their staffs anyway but some have a particularly important effect on the way schools are now to be managed.

1. The head is required to plan and state the overall aims, objectives and performance of his or her school – no more happy-go-lucky assumptions that we will muddle through.
2. The head is required to establish relationships with all concerned in the running of the school and with outside bodies such as the

PART VIII – Conditions of employment of head teachers

Overriding requirements

27. A head teacher shall carry out his professional duties in accordance with and subject to –

(1) the provisions of the Education Acts 1944 to 1988;

(2) any orders and regulations having effect thereunder;

(3) the articles of government of the school of which he is head teacher, to the extent to which their content is prescribed by statute;

(4) where the school is a voluntary school or a grant-maintained school which was formerly a voluntary school, any trust deed applying in relation thereto;

(5) any scheme of local management approved or imposed by the Secretary of State under section 34 of the Education Reform Act 1988**(a)**;

and, to the extent to which they are not inconsistent with these conditions –

(a) provisions of the articles of government the content of which is not so prescribed;

(b) in the case of a school which has a delegated budget,

(i) any rules, regulations or policies laid down by the governing body under their powers as derived from any of the sources specified in sub-paragraphs (1) to (5) and (a) above; and

(ii) any rules, regulations or policies laid down by his employers with respect to matters for which the governing body is not so responsible;

(c) in any other case, any rules, regulations or policies laid down by his employers; and

(d) the terms of his appointment.

General functions

28. Subject to paragraph 27 above, the head teacher shall be responsible for the internal organisation, management and control of the school.

Consultation 29. In carrying out his duties the head teacher shall consult, where this is appropriate, with the authority, the governing body, the staff of the school and the parents of its pupils.

Professional duties

30. The professional duties of a head teacher shall include –

School aims (1) formulating the overall aims and objectives of the school and policies for their implementation;

(a) 1988 c.40.

Appointment of staff

(2) participating in the selection and appointment of the teaching and non-teaching staff of the school;

Management of staff

(3) (a) deploying and managing all teaching and non-teaching staff of the school and allocating particular duties to them (including such duties of the head teacher as may properly be delegated to the deputy head teacher or other members of the staff) in a manner consistent with their conditions of employment, maintaining a reasonable balance for each teacher between work carried out in school and work carried out elsewhere;

(b) ensuring that the duty of providing cover for absent teachers is shared equitably among all teachers in the school (including the head teacher), taking account of their teaching and other duties;

Liaison with staff unions and associations

(4) maintaining relationships with organisations representing teachers and other persons on the staff of the school;

Curriculum

(5) (a) determining, organising and implementing an appropriate curriculum for the school, having regard to the needs, experience, interests, aptitudes and stage of development of the pupils and the resources available to the school; and his duty under sections 1(1) and 10(1)(b) and (2) of the Education Reform Act 1988(**a**);

(b) securing that all pupils in attendance at the school take part in daily collective worship in pursuance of his duty under section 10(1)(a) of the Education Reform Act 1988;

Review

(6) keeping under review the work and organisation of the school;

Standards of teaching and learning

(7) evaluating the standards of teaching and learning in the school, and ensuring that proper standards of professional performance are established and maintained;

Appraisal, training and development of staff

(8) (a) supervising and participating in arrangements made in accordance with regulations made under section 40 of the Education (No. 2) Act 1986 (**b**) for the appraisal of the performance of teachers in the school; participating in arrangements made for the appraisal of his performance as head teacher, and that of other head teachers who are the responsibility of the same appraising body in accordance with such regulations; participating in the identification of areas in which he would benefit from further training and undergoing such training;

(b) ensuring that all staff in the school have access to advice and training appropriate to their needs, in accordance with the policies of the maintaining authority or, in the case of a grant-maintained school, of the governing body, for the development of staff;

Management information

(9) providing information about the work and performance of the staff employed at the school where this is relevant to their future employment;

Pupil progress

(10) ensuring that the progress of the pupils of the school is monitored and recorded;

Pastoral care

(11) determining and ensuring the implementation of a policy for the pastoral care of the pupils;

Discipline

(12) determining, in accordance with any written statement of general principles provided for him by the governing body, measures to be

---

(**a**) 1988 c.40.
(**b**) 1986 c.61.

taken with a view to promoting, among the pupils, self-discipline and proper regard for authority, encouraging good behaviour on the part of the pupils, securing that the standard of behaviour of the pupils is acceptable and otherwise regulating the conduct of the pupils; making such measures generally known within the school, and ensuring that they are implemented;

(13) ensuring the maintenance of good order and discipline at all times during the school day (including the midday break) when pupils are present on the school premises and whenever the pupils are engaged in authorised school activities, whether on the school premises or elsewhere;

Relations with parents

(14) making arrangement for parents to be given regular information about the school curriculum, the progress of their children and other matters affecting the school, so as to promote common understanding of its aims;

Relations with other bodies

(15) promoting effective relationships with persons and bodies outside the school;

Relations with governing body

(16) advising and assisting the governing body of the school in the exercise of its functions, including (without prejudice to any rights he may have as a governor of the school) attending meetings of the governing body and making such reports to it in connection with the discharge of his functions as it may properly require either on a regular basis or from time to time;

Relations with authority

(17) (except in the case of grant-maintained schools) providing for liaison and co-operation with the officers of the maintaining authority; making such reports to the authority in connection with the discharge of his functions as it may properly require, either on a regular basis or from time to time;

Relations with other educational establishments

(18) maintaining liaison with other schools and further education establishments with which the school has a relationship;

Resources

(19 allocating, controlling and accounting for those financial and material resources of the school which are under the control of the head teacher;

Premises

(20) making arrangements, if so required by the maintaining authority or the governing body of a grant-maintained school (as appropriate), for the security and effective supervision of the school buildings and their contents and of the school grounds; and ensuring (if so required) that any lack of maintenance is promptly reported to the maintaining authority or, if appropriate, the governing body;

Absence

(21) arranging for a deputy head teacher or other suitable person to assume responsibility for the discharge of his functions as head teacher at any time when he is absent from the school;

Teaching

(22) participating, to such extent as may be appropriate having regard to his other duties, in the teaching of pupils at the school, including the provision of cover for absent teachers.

Daily break

31. A head teacher shall be entitled to a break of reasonable length in the course of each school day, and shall arrange for a suitable person to assume responsibility for the discharge of his functions as head teacher during that break.

Figure 7 Contract of service for head

LEA, appropriate primary and secondary schools and colleges of FE. Perhaps above all there must be good working relationships with the governing body – certainly no more ivory towers.

3 The head is required to manage the staff, initiate disciplinary measures if necessary yet see that in aspects such as their work and cover they are treated fairly. The quality of their performance must be ensured. They must be appraised and given opportunities for training and professional development. Their representatives from professional associations must be consulted.

4 The head is required to communicate with governors and the LEA and parents are entitled to consultation and a great deal of information.

5 The head is required to see that the curriculum is properly organised and is appropriate for the needs of pupils and that daily collective worship is arranged. He or she must take part in teaching and cover.

6 The head is required to set standards of behaviour and see that these are maintained. There must be proper provision for pastoral care but, strangely, there is no direct reference to a responsibility for seeing that on grounds of safety there should be a proper system of pupil supervision.

7 The head is required to take responsibility for finance and premises. Both have a major impact on school management.

Most of these were previously professional obligations – they are now legal requirements under contract. Mr Lancaster should beware – he has great scope but is open to criticism and attack from many quarters and on many aspects. If in his attempts to ginger things up he fails to treat staff reasonably, ignores directed time, dismisses problems out of hand, fails to establish and maintain good relationships, does not provide information or makes inappropriate changes to the curriculum or teaching methods then he will find himself in real difficulty.

Deputies

The *Blue Book* Part IX has little to say of deputy heads, though in many ways they have the most difficult task to perform in schools. They work under the same conditions as assistant teachers with the added provisos that they must carry out additional responsibilities allocated by the head and deputise in the head's absence (see Figure 8).

PART IX – Conditions of employment of deputy head teachers

Professional duties

32. A person appointed deputy head teacher in a school, in addition to carrying out the professional duties of a school teacher, including those duties particularly assigned to him by the head teacher, shall –

(1) assist the head teacher in managing the school or such part of it as may be determined by the head teacher;

(2 undertake any professional duty of the head teacher which may be delegated to him by the head teacher;

(3) undertake, in the absence of the head teacher and to the extent required by him or the relevant body or, in the case of an aided school, the governing body, the professional duties of the head teacher;

(4) be entitled to a break of reasonable length in the course of each school day.

Figure 8 Contract of service for deputies

Appraisal

In most areas of employment staff appraisal is common enough. In teaching it is in its infancy and is treated with considerable suspicion by many heads and other teachers. Nevertheless, it is now a legal requirement.

Under S.35 the *Blue Book* requires as a condition of service that teachers be appraised. The requirements are contained in the Education (School Teacher Appraisal) Regulations 1991, which is a Statutory Instrument and therefore legally binding, guidance being given in DFE Circular 12/91, entitled *School Teacher Appraisal*.

The appraising body, as it is known, is the LEA for maintained schools and the governors in the case of those which are grant maintained. The governors of all these schools are responsible for seeing that a policy is adopted over appraisal and that this is reviewed from time to time. Appraisal for all covered by the legislation must be in progress by 1/9/95.

The aim, as expressed, is to help teachers to realise their potential and carry out their duties more effectively. Appraisal is not to form part of grievance or disciplinary procedures or dismissal. It applies to qualified teachers who are working for at least 40% of full time under a contract of at least one year and in one particular school. Consequently, probationers, articled or licensed teachers, supply staff, unqualified teachers and peripatetic teachers are not included. A record must be kept for each teacher appraised.

The appraisal cycle must normally be over two years with a review meeting held in the second year. If the teacher changes post then the cycle begins again. If internal promotion takes place then, at the head's discretion, the cycle may be re-commenced.For assistants the head appoints the appraiser but the teacher may request an alternative appointee. For heads there must be two appraisers, nominated by the appraising body; one of these must be a serving or ex-head who has experience of the same sector of education.

The appraisal should include classroom observation, an interview, a statement and a review. In the case of heads and other senior staff there should be an observation of management tasks carried out as a normal part of duties. If the appraiser asks others for information as part of the process then the person appraised must be made aware of this.

The statement of appraisal itself must not be produced by the appraiser alone. It must be produced in consultation with the person being appraised and he or she has the right to add any further comments in writing. Targets for action are listed in a separate annex. The statement for assistants is available only to the appraiser, the subject, the head and any review officer later appointed. The LEA and chair of governors may request to see the targets only. For heads both the LEA and the chair of governors should receive a copy of the entire statement.

The statements are confidential and are not available to governors generally. However, they may be used by those with a right of access to them, for example the head, in advising on discipline, dismissal, pay or promotion. However, there must be no direct link involved. Use in this way merits caution.

There should be a procedure for dealing with complaints against appraisal and arrangements for an impartial review officer to be appointed.

Once the appraisal has been completed all documents relating to it, except the statement itself, should be destroyed. When a new statement is prepared the previous one should be kept for three months in case a review has to take place.

Once the process of appraisal is entered into, it is likely that there will be further minor changes. School managers should keep a wary eye on the latest edition of the *Blue Book* and DFE pronouncements.

Scotland

Pay and conditions for Scottish teachers are negotiated by the Scottish Joint Negotiating Committee for Teaching Staff in School Education which has representatives of the Secretary of State for Scotland, Education Authorities and the Associations of the teachers. Details are to be found in the various Circulars issued by the committee. The English conditions are not applicable.

Ginger Man – a last word

From the little we have been told Mr Lancaster seems to be heading for trouble. Most of his stated intentions are legitimate ones. He is entitled to review staffing structures, incentive allowances and responsibilities but not to make fundamental changes without consent. If he does so then we may be talking of appeals to governors, grievance procedures or actions for constructive dismissal. He may review teaching groups and methods. He may set up meetings and make attendance compulsory in directed time. He may investigate absence. He may seek better standards of preparation and marking. He may not insist on participation in out-of-school activities unless this can be managed in directed time. However, he needs to remember that while legal obligations may be used to coerce staff, their limitations may be used as defensive weapons against arbitrary and ill-judged management decisions.

There may very well be a serious need for change but for Mr Lancaster to decide after one week that he knows the changes that are needed is presumptuous. Perhaps he has been encouraged to take urgent action by certain governors or officers of the LEA. If so, he should resist, for once in post he cannot easily be removed.

He needs to spend some time assessing the performance of staff and pupils and the efficiency of organisation and routine. He needs to absorb the atmosphere. First impressions may be wrong. Changes should only be made where necessary and what is good should be left alone. Most teachers take a professional pride in their work and recognise changes for the better. They are likely to support his changes if they will improve the quality of the school's performance but not if they are designed to illustrate his authority and ambition. They will appreciate his efforts to deal with those staff whose performance is below standard since they always cause problems for colleagues.

Mr Lancaster has to make his own judgments, consult with staff generally – not just with any hierarchy that exists – and gauge the attitudes of governors and parents. He will then be in a position to initiate change. As far as staffing problems are concerned he will need to deal with them at a personal level if at all possible. If not, then he will need to go to his governors confident that the law is on his side and armed with positive evidence and measured advice. He may then expect their backing.

Test yourself

1 The Governors of an all-girls school advertise for two mistresses – one to teach PE and the other to teach history. Is there any discrimination here?

2 The governors of a voluntary aided school offer a post orally to Mr A after interview and he accepts. Is there a legally binding contract made?

3 Mrs B, against the head's wishes, states her intention of applying for a post at another school and asks for a reference but the head refuses. Can Mrs B insist?

4 Candidates for a headship are asked at interview if they intend to move and live in the area. Is this a legitimate question?

5 School C has no additional incentive allowances to give yet it wishes to retain an excellent teacher. What can it do?

6 Mrs D has a timetable mostly of English, with some GCSE work plus a few periods of geography. After returning from a lengthy maternity leave she is given a timetable consisting mainly of geography with some English but no GCSE classes. She is angry and resigns, claiming constructive dismissal. What is the position?

7 The head grants Mr E a day's compassionate leave of absence with pay to attend the funeral of his cousin. Without contacting the head Mr E takes two further days off to help his cousin's widow cope with her affairs. What are your comments?

8 Must details of directed time be given to staff when the head is sure that all school activities can be contained within the 1265 hours?

9 Mrs F has been teaching for nearly 30 years and will not suffer the indignity of appraisal. She would rather resign. Must she be forced to comply?

10 Is this a reasonable instruction by the head?

In the interests of good discipline, particularly with regard to older boys, lady members of staff are directed not to wear the very high mini-skirts now in fashion.

Comments will be found at the end of the book (page 201).

Further reading

Croner's Head's Legal Guide (1992), published by Croner, is a mine of information relating to the employment of teachers. Other sources would be the handbooks of teacher associations and general works on employment law. The author's own *Know Your Rights – Teachers*, Neil Adams (1991), published in the 'How To' series, gives a concise guide. A close examination of the *Blue Book* would be useful.

8 Managing staff – discipline, grievances and union action

Discipline

In a well-run and happy school there will be few serious problems of staff discipline. Most will be minor matters that can be settled quickly and with little fuss. Major incidents or confrontations are so rare that heads are often at a loss to know the action to be taken and correct procedures to be followed. Governors now have the power to deal with staff disciplinary matters and many will be in difficulty – there have been several cases already of governors mishandling such matters. They will be looking to the head for guidance.

Serious disciplinary situations may arise for a variety of reasons. There could be a defiant or negligent repetition of minor infringements; there could be flagrant breaches of contract; there could be acts threatening the safety of pupils or colleagues; there could be violent, abusive or indecent behaviour; there could be abuse of authority or disclosure of confidential information; there could be misuse of the employer's property; there could be the commission of a criminal offence relevant to the holding of a position of trust such as that of a teacher. The list is not exhaustive.

In Chapter 6 we saw that it is normal for employers to draw up a code of disciplinary procedures. Not only is this necessary to establish fairness for both sides in situations where disciplinary action may be involved, but the use of agreed procedures is evidence of fair treatment in claims for unfair dismissal.

Since the introduction of LMS the governing body of each school is responsible for deciding on disciplinary procedures for its own establishment. It would be wise to adopt those agreed between LEAs and teacher unions since these will be the result of considerable thought and consultation. Otherwise governors must set up their own consultative machinery. The procedures in being will be based on the Code recommended by ACAS but it is important to remember that there may well be local variations.

The transfer of responsibility for staffing matters (including discipline) to governors has created an additional problem, even if they have decided to adopt the standard procedures agreed previously with the LEA. There must be provision for appeals against disciplinary decisions and governors must hear them. Since it would be unjust for those meting out the punishment to deal with an appeal against it, one group must deal with the first hearing and a different one be left to handle the appeal.

There are a number of points to remember over the procedures:

1 On appointment employees are entitled to receive a copy of the procedures.

2 The aim of procedures is to try to put matters right and give advice and help where possible.

3 The pattern of warnings should be set out clearly.

4 Positive evidence should be produced to justify the action proposed.

5 Before action is taken, employees should be given a chance to put their side of the matter.

6 The employee should be allowed to be accompanied by a 'friend' – usually a union representative – when a warning is given.

7 No employee should be dismissed for a first disciplinary offence unless gross misconduct is involved.

8 There should be a right of appeal against disciplinary action and a clear indication of how this is to be dealt with.

9 Where warnings are recorded there should be a right to have them removed after a stated period of satisfactory conduct.

Short of actual dismissal, disciplinary action against teachers or other staff will take the form of warnings. As explained in Chapter 6, these will usually be **informal**, **formal** or **final**. For relatively trivial matters the informal warning may indicate that official notice has been taken of the unacceptable behaviour – almost certainly there will have been some previous mention of it – and unless things improve there will be a further progression through disciplinary procedures. A formal warning means that the matter is now serious and unless it is put right a final warning may be given and this may lead to dismissal. According to the seriousness of the matter the disciplinary action may commence at any stage. A final warning may be given immediately for something not quite meriting instant dismissal. For gross misconduct dismissal would be appropriate and no warnings are necessary. What constitutes gross misconduct is debatable. Examples from cases that qualify include betrayal of trust and sexual relations with pupils (even if the pupil has reached the age of consent); violent attacks on pupils or colleagues; the falsification of examination results; or the commission of theft.

It is usual for both informal or formal warnings to be given by the head and for the committee of the governors to give final warnings or decide on dismissal. If the head gives a warning there should be a witness present, say the deputy or head of department concerned, and the opportunity given for the employee to have a friend present. If a formal warning is given then it should be followed up in writing and the record placed on the employee's file. If governors make the decision then this should be in line with clearly-stated policy.

If gross misconduct is alleged then it is likely that it will be embarrassing, or even dangerous, for the employee to remain at work. The head or the governors have the power to suspend the employee until the investigation is complete and a decision reached. Only the governors can order re-instatement. An employee on suspension must be given full pay until the result of the hearing and any appeal is reached.

We can now see how disciplinary procedures might be applied in certain situations:

Incident

Parental complaints have been received over the marking of exercise books by a certain member of staff.

Comment

This is almost the classic example of when to use the full range of warnings. If investigation supports the complaints then an informal warning is appropriate, followed by advice and close monitoring. If there is some improvement but the marking is still not satisfactory then a formal warning should follow. If there is clearly a deliberate refusal to comply in any way then that stage might be skipped and a final warning given. If the marking is still below standard after a formal warning then a final warning and eventual dismissal can follow.

Cases like this are likely to be lengthy and entail a great deal of monitoring and recording but that is necessary if a solution is to be found. Written evidence in the form of unmarked books, monitoring reports and parental complaints is important. The last may be difficult to obtain since many parents are afraid of victimisation of pupils if they complain in writing but if they will do so it gives greater support to the head when going to the governors.

Incident

A piece of electrical apparatus has been found to be faulty. It has been withdrawn from use and is in a store cupboard awaiting collection for repair. Staff have been informed that it must not be used. Although he knows this a teacher takes it from the cupboard and allows a pupil to use it. The pupil receives a shock and has to be taken to hospital.

Comment

This teacher knows the possible danger, has disobeyed instructions and put a child at serious risk. There is a clear breach of contract here and negligence – possibly even the prospect of a prosecution under Health and Safety regulations. The misconduct here could merit dismissal or at the very least a final warning.

Incident

Mr Van Winkle has been late for school on two or three occasions. Each time the lateness has only been for a few minutes but his class has been left unsupervised briefly. He has never offered an excuse or apology. When tackled by the head he says that his wife has left him and that he sleeps very heavily. Matters improve for a short time but then the trouble begins all over again.

Comment

This may sound a trivial matter for which an informal warning is the most that is required. However, to leave pupils unsupervised always constitutes a risk. If this is a secondary school the risk is not so great, because of the age of pupils, unless the room is a potentially dangerous place such as a laboratory or workshop. If the incident took place in a primary school with very young children then the risk is so much greater. Depending on the exact circumstances an informal or formal warning would seem appropriate. This teacher appears to have domestic problems and some counselling and discussion of his difficulties might help, but he should be made aware of the risks he is taking. Mr Van Winkle may be one of those teachers who come late but are prepared to give a great deal of valuable time voluntarily after school. That creates a case for tactful handling by the head.

Incident

A girl pupil alleges that a school caretaker has fondled her breasts. He denies this but admits that he has been over-friendly towards the

girl and says that she has made obvious advances towards him, which he rejected. Her parents say that they realise there could be a prosecution but they do not wish this to happen because of the effect of a court appearance on their daughter.

Comment

This is the most difficult of situations to handle because of the conflicting statements. Staff do lie in desperate situations and pupils do concoct stories about teachers and other staff.

The caretaker needs to be suspended pending the result of the investigation and informed of his rights. It would probably be better for the girl to be questioned at home in the presence of her parents and remain away from school for a few days. Careful and objective evidence needs to be sought from the two persons concerned and from any reliable witnesses. The head must then go to the disciplinary committee of the governors with his report. The caretaker's side should be heard and the governors would do well to speak to the girl with her parents present. They must then decide what action to take.

If they believe the girl then dismissal for gross misconduct must take place and the caretaker may appeal. If he loses then there is still the possibility of his claim for unfair dismissal. If they believe the caretaker then they must order his re-instatement. However, since he has admitted being over-friendly with a girl pupil a warning of at least formal level could be given regarding his behaviour towards girls in the school.

The parents here did not wish a prosecution to take place and presumably have not informed the police. The head is certainly at liberty to do so and after their investigation the local Crown Prosecutor might decide to prosecute in spite of the conflicting statements and the unwillingness of the parents.

Dismissal

This is the final disciplinary action to be taken by governors, either as the employer or as agent of the employer. All the safeguards mentioned earlier of the use of disciplinary procedures and a properly constituted appeals procedure apply and need careful thought. A further difficulty may arise.

An LEA cannot prevent a governing body from dismissing an employee and it must pay any compensation that may be awarded for unfair dismissal awarded by an industrial tribunal unless it can demonstrate that the governors have acted unreasonably or unfairly. If there is unreasonable or unfair handling of the situation the LEA may then deduct the amount of the compensation from the school's budget. The governors might think it worthwhile to be a few thousand pounds short in some cases but if re-instatement has been ordered and refused the final financial blow could be a heavy one. The governors need to keep in touch with the LEA when final warnings or dismissal are contemplated.

There is little evidence yet as to what constitutes unreasonable or unfair behaviour on the part of governors but some are obvious – a lack of disciplinary procedures, no offer of advice or help to the employee or no proper handling of appeals, would be examples. Dismissal then should be approached with care but should certainly be used where it is deserved.

Grievance procedures

Disciplinary procedures involve the employer, or the governors or head acting for the employer, taking action for an employee's misconduct. What if there is alleged misconduct on the part of the employer, the employer's agent or fellow employees? Such situations are covered by a system of grievance procedures. While an employer may dispense with disciplinary procedures at his peril there is a legal requirement for grievance procedures under the Contracts of Employment Act 1972. For teachers the model procedures will be found in Appendix 2(1) of the *Burgundy Book*. There is a separate provision for heads. As a result of the Education Reform Act of 1988, governors are required to set up both disciplinary and grievance procedures. Again, they would be wise to adopt those previously agreed.

Mr Irving has been on the standard scale as a teacher of English for a number of years. He does not get on well with his head of department and recently has had a heated argument with him over the use of American texts in the English syllabus. An extra incentive allowance is to be given to the English department and the head of department recommends that this should go to Mr Washington, a highly promising young teacher who has been on the staff for only two years. The head wants to keep Mr Washington on the staff and so he agrees. The governors accept the recommendation. Mr Irving is hurt and angry. He feels that he has been treated badly by the head of department, the head and the governors. What can he do?

Since there is no evidence of unlawful discrimination here he must turn to his grievance procedures, a copy of which should have been given to him on appointment. The aim of such procedures is to allow individual employees – not groups – to complain where they feel there is unfair treatment which is not covered by any other aspect of employment law. So Mr Irving might declare a grievance against his colleague for deliberately not recommending him for promotion. He might delcare a grievance against the head for not giving him fair consideration and against the governors for the same reason.

Any employee in a school may declare a grievance against any other employee, the head or the governors.

Mr Irving may feel that on grounds of length of service he should have received the incentive allowance rather than it being given to Mr Washington. That alone is not a genuine grievance. Length of service is only one factor in deciding on internal promotion and the governors were entitled to award the allowance to Mr Washington if they believed that to be appropriate and in the best interests of the school. Mr Irving's genuine grievance is that as a long-serving member of staff he was entitled to be given fair consideration for internal promotion and this has not happened.

It could have been achieved by internal interview when both teachers, and perhaps others, would have been able to put forward their own merits and the head and governors, taking all factors into consideration, would have been able to decide. In Mr Irving's case the right decision may have been made but it was made unfairly.

The main points common in grievance procedures are:

1. An attempt should be made to settle grievances informally.
2. The person with a grievance should be granted an early interview.
3. If these methods fail to settle the problem then the grievance should be put in writing to the employer.
4. The head should then submit a report to the governors.
5. The governors should hold an early meeting to consider the report.
6. There should be a right of appeal as agreed under the procedures.
7. There should be a right for the employee to have a union representative present at any stage.

The similar conditions for the head to pursue grievances against governors or the LEA are also in the *Burgundy Book* Appendix 2(1).

Collective disputes

These occur when a group of employees, usually from a particular union, have a dispute with the employer. There are procedures to deal with such situations. The model for such procedures is to be found in the *Burgundy Book* Appendix 2(2).

To date, such disputes have almost always concerned disagreements across an authority over aspects of conditions of service but there are isolated instances of the staff of individual schools being involved, for example over a governors' decision to re-admit suspended pupils. With the spread of LMS perhaps individual schools will be involved to a greater extent. When a collective dispute is in prospect staff need union advice and backing, so does the head. Governors need to consult the LEA. Grant maintained schools will need to consult the DFE and their own organisation, the Grant Maintained Schools Trust.

Union action

Members of the National Union of Pedagogues are in dispute over a pay claim by teachers. A national ballot has been taken and support given for strike action. Even the staff of Sleepy Hollow Primary School are affected since there are six union members who are assistant staff and a seventh who does not belong to a union at all. The six are instructed to strike on a certain day and thereafter only to work in directed time. Due notice of the action is given to the head, Mr Ichabod Crane. The seventh member of staff asks Mr Crane what she should do.

At the time of writing such incidents are likely to be rare but in the mid-eighties they were common enough, at times on a weekly or even a daily basis. They had a serious impact on the management of schools. The difficulties could arise again. How should Mr Crane handle the situation?

Heads tend to react to such incidents with anger and frustration at the disruption to be caused. They often see such actions as personal attacks on themselves. Such feelings, though perhaps natural enough, should be resisted and suppressed in the interests of future harmony and good working relationships.

Providing it is allowed by current legislation – and this is liable to change at any time – employees may take industrial action, even though technically they are in breach of contract, without any reprisals except loss of salary. Like all other employees, teachers are entitled to belong to a union or not to do so if they wish. If they are members then they are bound to follow decisions properly taken or resign. Industrial action is a legitimate right and may indeed be the only way of gaining fair treatment.

First Mr Crane should consult his own union and ask for guidance on his own position. He should then consider as objectively as possible the safety and welfare of his pupils, the rights of his staff and the need for clear communication to parents. Once he has made provisional plans to cover the disruption he should consult with the union concerned. This could be with the staff representative – in a large school it would have to be with all union representatives. In his case there could easily be consultation with all six teachers. He should emphasise that, while understanding their position, his main consideration is for the safety and welfare of pupils, a view which he is sure they will share.

He should then explain his provisional plans and invite their comments as to how these might be altered or improved. Hopefully, he will then obtain a consensus but whether he does so or not, after consultation with the chair of governors, he must make firm decisions. Those decisions and exact details of the organisation involved should then be communicated simply to all staff, parents and governors and in good time. In Mr Crane's case this will almost certainly mean closure for at least one session.

The teacher who is not a union member should be asked to report for duty as normal. She should not be asked to teach or supervise pupils normally taught by those on strike but if her commitment is to one class for the entire duration of the strike and if break supervision can be provided then there is no reason why the school should not remain open for that class. Otherwise, she may be given any reasonable non-teaching duties.

Where a number of unions are represented in a school then those not on strike may be asked to carry out normal duties but not those of staff on strike. Non-teaching staff should not be asked to undertake duties normally carried out by teachers on strike.

The intention of staff only to work in directed time could be a blow to out-of-school activities but Mr Crane cannot compel them to do otherwise. Hopefully, he has made out a management plan for directed time so that the essentials of teaching, supervision, meetings and consultation with parents are allowed for.

If Mr Crane consults, makes clear and sensible decisions and communicates them in good time to all concerned then the risk of repercussions and further bad feeling will be reduced.

Further reading

Those works recommended at the end of the last chapter are useful for this section also. In addition an examination of the relevant procedures for discipline and grievances would be valuable.

9 Managing pupils – negligence and supervision

Mrs Wordsworth's Diary

Mrs Wordsworth is head of Lower School at Lakeland High School. She has responsibility for all aspects of pastoral care and discipline for some 400 pupils. She is an ambitious woman and is studying for the Advanced Diploma in Educational Management of the Open University. As part of a research project she has to keep a diary recording incidents dealt with during a particular week. Here are some extracts from her rough notes:

Monday After assembly officious Lucy arrived with class register of 9Z. Mr Coleridge had not arrived to mark it ('Yet again,' smirked Lucy) and she had taken it upon herself to mark it. Warned her not to do this again and checked with the class to find that the entries were correct. Coleridge on patrol duty during break but found him in staff room corner smoking a vile-smelling cigarette. Tackled him over neglecting his class and failing in patrol duty. Profuse apologies, of course. Lives in a dream world that man.

Alice Fell reported yet again for disrupting English lesson by persistent talking.

Tuesday Mary Hutchinson fell from climbing frame in gym. Ambulance called as fracture suspected. Phone call and letter to parents and accident recorded.

Alice again. This time reported for bringing CD player to school against rules. Player confiscated and letter to parents – yet again.

Another accident. Simon Lee fell in playground and cut his hand on glass from broken bottle. Cut looked nasty so sent to hospital for checking. Parents contacted. Caretaker told of glass and incident reported to deputy.

Wednesday Geography trip to Windermere by school minibus. John Langdale had failed to bring parental consent but was desperate to go. Managed to contact mother who had lost the form but gave her consent over phone.

Alice once more – this time for fighting with other girls in the toilets. Not her fault, of course. 'What do you do, miss, when they call you slag?' Efforts to get her parents into school to discuss problems still unsuccessful.

Meeting with welfare officer to discuss attendance problems of W.W. and S.C. Asked him to visit homes of both and identify any particular problems.

Mary OK. Simon needed a couple of stitches.

Thursday Mr Southey, in charge of yesterday's trip, reported that Jenny Duddon had passed out while walking up the side of a hill near the lake. She recovered quickly and seemed all right but another member of staff had taken her back to the minibus to rest. Later she told him that she had these blackouts occasionally and had seen the doctor. Mr Southey unaware of this and nothing in my records. Parents contacted.

Friday The last straw with Alice! She had a pocket knife and was threatening other girls, who reported her. Head agreed to exclude her for three school days and demand that parents come in or indefinite exclusion would be considered.

Head also revealed that Simon Lee's parents had been to see him regarding incident with broken glass. Someone has told them they 'have rights' and the term negligence keeps cropping up.

Final blow. Michael Shepherd comes in tears at 4 o'clock and says that Miss Dove has slapped him in the face in front of the whole class and for no reason at all. Knowing him there'll be a reason but promise to look into it. Miss Dove already left so matter remains till Monday. TGIF.

Any reader who has had experience of working in a middle management role in a school will be familiar with most of the incidents recorded here. All require some grasp of the legal implications involved. This chapter and the next will deal with these.

In loco parentis

From Mrs Wordsworth's diary we can see that for the duration of the school day, and perhaps beyond it, teachers are taking responsibility for minors; that is, they are standing in place of parents and must act accordingly. This means that school managers not only have to be aware of employment law, as discussed in the last few chapters, but they must also be conscious of the common law as it affects those who act as parent substitutes.

The concept of *in loco parentis* does not only apply to teachers, it also affects anyone standing in place of parents – social workers, staff in residential homes, caretakers, welfare assistants, clerical staff, midday supervisors, laboratory technicians, child-minders, even friends and neighbours. The difference for teachers is that they have received specialist training of a specific nature. In the light of that training, they must show a higher degree of care in relation to school activities and the handling of large groups of pupils.

The standard of that duty of care is difficult to define since it is based on the concept of what a good, responsible parent might or might not do. Notions regarding that may well change over the years. There is no statute law on the subject and so conclusions have to be drawn from decided cases.

The basic definition is provided in *Williams v Eady 1893*:

> **'As to the law on the subject there can be no doubt . . . that the schoolmaster was bound to take such care of his boys as a careful father would take of his boys and there could not be a better definition of the duty of a schoolmaster.'**

This disarmingly simple statement begs questions as to what constitutes a careful parent and what such a person does or does not do. Each situation will be different; a succession of cases over the years has helped to clarify certain aspects. They have dealt with a wide range of incidents involving PE equipment and activities, scissors and knives, paper clips and bamboo arrows, oil-cans and crackers, broken bottles and heaps of coke on playgrounds, golf balls and trampette elastic, vitriol, a cricket roller, unguarded machines and cookers, school buses, rough play and sliding, rugby tackles by staff, poking a staffroom fire or making tea for staff, the early arrival of pupils or their early dismissal. In all these cases the point at issue was whether the supervision was adequate or not.

The impact of a list like this might cause teachers to think that children must be protected at all times and that no risks of any kind should ever be taken. This is not so. In good homes children are often at risk and accidents will happen. Most injuries that take place in schools do not lead to court actions at all. Many brought on the aspects listed above failed because the court considered that teachers had done all that could reasonably be expected of them. Teachers who carry out their responsibilities sensibly and with reasonable care have little to worry about.

From *Wray v Essex C.C. 1936*:

> **'I do not think anybody is responsible for this unfortunate mischance, which appears to me to be pure misadventure . . . there is**

nothing which the master could or ought to have foreseen . . . he committed no breach of duty towards the plaintiff.'

And from *Jones v London C.C. 1932*:

'The plaintiff had undoubtedly suffered serious injury but it does not follow that because he suffered an injury that therefore he can get compensation from anybody: he has to show some breach of a legal duty which entitles him to recover compensation.'

And from *Hudson v Governors of Rotherham Grammar School 1938*:

'These things have got to be treated as matters of commonsense not to put on Mr Johnson (the teacher) any higher standard of care than that of a reasonably careful parent.
If boys were kept in cotton wool some of them would choke themselves with it. They would manage to have accidents. We always did, members of the jury – we did not always have actions at law afterwards.
You have to consider whether or not you would expect a headmaster to exercise such a degree of care that boys could never get into mischief. Has any reasonable parent yet succeeded in exercising such care as to prevent a boy getting into mischief and, if he did, what sort of boys should we produce?'

Finally, we might mention the judge in a case involving a playground accident who commented that although teachers have a duty to take reasonable care of pupils they are not required to impose a regime which 'suppresses natural high spirits'.

The concept of the prudent or careful parent is mentioned in case after case and in each the judge has to decide what that imaginary parent might have done or might not have done in the particular situation. That is one problem. There are two others of importance.

Professional training

The responsibility of parents is in family circumstances and they are not expected to have any particular expertise as a result of training. Teachers are trained to deal with pupils in a variety of situations, ranging from ordinary classroom control to the management of potentially dangerous situations in laboratories, workshops and gymnasia. How can the concept of the careful parent then be applied? The judge in *Lyes v Middlesex C.C. 1962* made an effort:

'I hold that the standard is that of a reasonably prudent parent judged not in the context of his own home but in that of a school,

in other words, a person exhibiting the responsible mental qualities of a prudent parent in the circumstances of school life.'

He seems to be suggesting that when applying the careful parent concept you have to imagine the parent to have been given the teacher's training and then placed in the particular situation. Another complex problem for a judge.

Numbers

Parents deal with only a few children at a time. Teachers deal with entire classes and senior staff may have to make decisions affecting hundreds of pupils. How can the idea of the careful parent be applied to such large groups? The judge in *Beaumont V Surrey C.C. 1968* said:

> **'. . . it is a headmaster's duty, bearing in mind the propensities of boys and indeed girls between the ages of eleven and 17 and 18, to take all reasonable and proper steps to prevent any of the pupils under his care from suffering injury from inanimate objects, from the actions of their fellow pupils, or from a combination of the two. That is a high standard.'**

This case concerned an incident involving a large group of pupils on a school playground. The decision in the Lyes case would say also that where large groups are concerned you imagine the careful parent who has the teacher's expertise and is placed in the particular situation. Difficult again.

Readers will have noticed that many of the cases quoted seem rather old. This is largely because the principles are well established and most incidents do not reach the courts. If the employer, who is of course vicariously liable, believes that the case is likely to be lost then there will be a settlement out of court in order to save costs. Only a parent who is really dissatisfied or vindictive, and who is prepared to take the considerable financial risk involved, is likely to go to law.

However, we can see that the concept of in *loco parentis* is still relevant today if we examine the latest case on record.

The caretaker and the shot

(The details of this case are to found in *Porter v Barking and Dagenham London B.C. Council and Another 1990.*)

Mr Chesney was the caretaker of a London school and his own son was a pupil there. After school one day he allowed his son and a friend, both aged fourteen, to take a shot and practise with it on school property. Mr Chesney had no authority to do this. An accident occurred, the friend was injured and an action was brought against the Council which was vicariously liable for Mr Chesney's alleged negligence. The case was dismissed.

The reason for the decision was stated to be that the duty of care owed by someone acting as a parent should not be applied to boys aged fourteen or over so overcautiously and in such a way as to stifle initiative and independence. The judge added that they were qualities which should be encouraged and boys should not be wholly mollycoddled. Mr Chesney had not fallen below the standard of a careful parent. One suspects that if javelins had been involved the result would have been different.

So all the staff mentioned in Mrs Wordsworth's diary are *in loco parentis*, including the head and the caretaker. If, as a result of their action or inaction, a pupil suffers harm then an action for negligence may be brought.

Negligence

The term 'negligence' has been used loosely on a number of occasions in this book already. In law it has a specific meaning. It is a tort – a civil wrong – for which the remedy is compensation in the form of money damages awarded by a civil court, though in certain rare extreme cases it may constitute a criminal offence. The aim is to compensate the injured party, as far as money may do so, for the harm that has been suffered.

The essence of the tort is that by careless action, or careless lack of it, the defendant has caused harm to the plaintiff (pursuer in Scotland). The harm is normally physical in the sense of injury and issues arising from that such as disablement, pain or inability to continue leading a normal life in some way. There has been a tendency in recent times to also consider damages for nervous shock or trauma. However, the courts have resisted attempts to gain damages for second-hand emotional shock, for example from relatives, other than close ones, of those dying in the Zeebrugge ferry disaster or the football tragedy at Sheffield who had witnessed the full horror of the event on television.

Proof

Contrary to popular opinion, it is a difficult and lengthy process to gain compensation for negligence through the courts under English law;

the situation in Scotland is virtually the same. This is largely because the burden of proof, while not as high as in criminal cases, is an onerous one and lies upon the plaintiff in the majority of cases.

A teacher who has had no training in life-saving is allowed to take a group of young children to a baths where there is no trained attendant on duty. He allows pupils to jump into the deep end and one of them is drowned. On these facts the parents of the child would not have to prove negligence, it is obvious. The court would declare such a case to be described as *res ipsa loquitur* (the thing speaks for itself) but would give the defendant a chance to put his side. Since there is unlikely to be a reasonable explanation such cases tend only to reach court if the parties cannot agree on the amount of compensation.

In most instances therefore the plaintiff has to prove the negligence. This consists of four elements.

1 Duty of care

First the plaintiff must show that a duty of care was owed by the defendant, i.e. that the latter had a responsibility to have in mind the welfare of the former. Mostly, we owe a duty of care towards anyone that we know, or ought to know, is likely to be affected by our conduct; this is known as the 'neighbour' test. The classic definition is to be found in *Donoghue v Stevenson 1932*:

> **'You must take reasonable care to avoid acts or omissions which you can reasonably foresee would be likely to injure your neighbour. Who, then, in law is my neighbour? The answer seems to be – persons who are so closely and directly affected by my act that I ought reasonably to have them in contemplation as being so affected when I am directing my mind to the acts or omissions which are called in question . . .'**

The standard of the duty of care will vary according to the circumstances of the 'neighbour'. It must take into account such factors as known vulnerability because of physical or medical conditions, or of age or intelligence. Clearly, all school staff owe a duty of care towards pupils on school premises and off them when they are in charge of school parties. That goes without saying, though that duty of care may differ according to the age of pupils or the nature of activities involved.

One question that may arise for schools is whether there is a duty of care towards trespassers. The basic answer is that there is not, though traps must not be set deliberately for them. However, the Occupier's Liability Act 1984 requires that if trespassing is known to take place, or is clearly likely to happen, then reasonable steps must be taken to prevent it. Warning notices might suffice for adults but where young children are involved good fencing and locked gates would be highly desirable.

Schools are particularly vulnerable and clear efforts need to be seen to be made to dissuade trespassers. Warnings on circulars to parents would help and direct letters to the parents of known trespassers. Evidence of reasonable steps to warn and deter trespassers may allow escape from liability for any injury that may occur.

2 Breach

Second, a plaintiff must show that the duty of care has been broken. This means not behaving as a reasonable person could be expected to behave in the circumstances. If you are driving along the road, carefully and within any speed limit, and a child suddenly runs out under the wheels of your car and is injured, then there will be no right to compensation since you are behaving reasonably and no action on your part could have prevented the accident – there is no breach and therefore no negligence. If you then drive away and make no effort to obtain help for the injured child then that is breach – no reasonable person should do that. It would also be a criminal matter.

For teachers, breach lies in not behaving as a good parent, who has had the benefit of professional training, would have done in the particular circumstances.

Those circumstances are important. In *Barnes v Hampshire C.C. 1969* an infant pupil was dismissed by her teacher five minutes before normal time and her mother, who was on her way to meet her, was unaware of the change. The child ran into the road and was injured. The action of the teacher was held to be breach since a good parent would not have allowed a very young child to venture alone into a busy road. It is likely that there would have been no breach if the pupil had been older and could be expected by a good parent to walk home alone.

In Mr Chesney's case the judge inferred that in his opinion a good parent would allow a 14-year-old boy to practise with a shot and so there was no breach.

Age can be an important factor then in deciding whether breach has occurred or not. So can the nature of the activity. To leave even older pupils alone in a workshop with dangerous equipment would certainly be breach but the same pupils left alone to study in a school library would not be so.

We can now consider some questions regarding the characters appearing in Mrs Wordsworth's diary.

Was Mr Coleridge in breach of his duty of care by leaving his class unattended and failing to carry out his patrol duty? Perhaps not in the first instance, if he was only a few moments late and the room did not contain dangerous equipment. But he runs a risk since there is always the danger of a group disturbance and these appear to be only year nine pupils. In the second instance there was breach – a large number of pupils milling round a school building requires patrolling staff to maintain order and deal with emergencies. He was, of course, in breach of contract on both counts.

Was there breach in the gym when Mary fell from the frame? If there was a trained PE teacher present who supervised properly and the frame was in good condition then this was a pure accident and no breach occurred.

Simon's hand was cut on broken glass. A responsible parent does not leave broken glass where children may be injured. There seems to be breach.

Jenny suffered a blackout on the school trip, received the attention of staff and recovered. No breach – but if she had not recovered quickly and the staff had not sought medical help then breach would certainly have occurred.

Apparently, Michael Shepherd has been slapped in the face by Miss Dove. Parents are still allowed under the law to punish their children and that includes reasonable corporal punishment. Since 1987, however, teachers have not been allowed to administer corporal punishment, except in independent schools, so Miss Dove may be in breach of her duty of care. This incident raises the whole issue of the use of physical force by teachers and will be dealt with in the next chapter.

3 Damage

The third element to be proved by a plaintiff is that of damage. Usually, there will be physical evidence of this in the form of personal physical damage or damage to property. If negligence is found, the court will also consider pain, suffering and loss involved and compensate for that as well.

Damage for emotional distress or nervous shock is difficult to prove because of the likely lack of physical evidence but both may certainly constitute the necessary element for a negligence action, as can proved financial loss for a negligent mis-statement.

At the Lakeland School there is no indication of damage caused by Mr Coleridge's behaviour; Jenny has suffered no harm; Mary has only suffered minor harm; Simon has certainly suffered harm and there appears to be breach; if Michael has been slapped then there is no sign of damage except to his feelings.

4 Reasonable foreseeability/Remoteness of damage

Finally, the plaintiff must show that the harm suffered was reasonably foreseeable. If it was not then the damage will be too remote for the court to take into account. This does not mean that the defendant must have known that the harm would occur but that, on grounds of reasonableness, should have realised that such an outcome could follow. If the harm was so remote that the defendant could not have foreseen it then there is no negligence.

In *Wright v Cheshire C.C. 1952* a group of boys was having a PE lesson in a gym and they were working in groups. The teacher was supervising by moving from one group to another. Roger Wright was with a group vaulting a buck with boys acting as support. Just as he set off to vault the bell went and one of the supporting boys turned and ran to the changing room. Roger fell and was seriously injured. The action for negligence was dismissed for a number of reasons but the court could easily have decided that the teacher could not have foreseen the sudden and inexplicable action of the supporting boy.

In *Affatu-Nartoy v Clark 1984* a teacher made a high tackle on a 15-year-old boy in a game of rugby. The court held that this was a breach of duty of care and could have added that it was reasonably foreseeable that damage might occur if a strong adult made such a tackle on a young boy.

In the Barnes case, mentioned above, the child was injured by a lorry. It was reasonably foreseeable that if a very young child is allowed onto a busy road by herself she may be knocked over. At the Lakeland School it was reasonably foreseeable that if broken glass was left on the playground someone might be injured by it. If Mr Coleridge had left his class unsupervised in a science laboratory and skylarking had led to a pupil being burned by acid then that would have been reasonably foreseeable.

Defences

Not only does the plaintiff normally have to prove the elements of negligence but the other party is able to put forward defences. Three of these may be relevant for schools and the first is certainly so.

This defence is known as consent. If a person consents to run a risk then negligence claims will not lie if the harm that results is clearly a consequence of taking that risk. By implication, all parents sending their children to school accept the normal risks of school life. PE is normally a compulsory part of the curriculum and parents understand the risks involved. *Affatu-Nartoy* illustrates the position well. The parents of a pupil tackled by another pupil in a rugby match can be assumed to have consented to the risks involved but not to those created by tackles from adults. Neither would parents consent to risks from broken glass in the playground.

The other possible defences are *inevitable accident* (where no one could have foreseen what might happen) and *necessity* (where harm is done in order to prevent a worse harm occurring).

Although not strictly a defence a defendant could argue that faced with several choices the action taken made sense at the time but turned out to be the wrong one in the light of subsequent developments. If that is accepted by the court than there is no negligence.

In *Lewis v Carmarthenshire C.C. 1955* a teacher decided to take two infants for a walk during the lunch break. She got them ready and told them to wait in a classroom while she went to the lavatory. On her way back she met another infant who had fallen and cut himself so she stopped and attended to him. She was away for about ten minutes but during that time the other two children had left the building. One attempted to cross the road in front of a lorry driven by Mr Lewis. He attempted to miss the child, crashed into a lamppost and was killed. The judge exonerated the teacher:

'Her duty was that of a careful parent. I cannot think that it could be considered negligent in a mother to leave a child dressed ready to go out with her for a few moments and then, if she found another of her children hurt and in need of immediate attention, she could be blamed for giving it, without thinking that the child who was waiting to go out with her might wander off into the street. It is very easy to be wise after the event and argue that she might have done this or that; but it seems to me that she acted just as one would expect her to do, that is to attend to the injured child first, never thinking that the one waiting for her would go off on his own.'

In this case however the LEA itself was not exonerated. It was found negligent because there was such easy access through the gates onto a busy main road.

Contributory negligence

In a negligence action a court may decide that both parties were at fault to some degree and adjust the compensation accordingly. This rarely applies to minors but might do so to a sixth former who understood the nature of a scientific experiment and deliberately disobeyed instructions, even if the teacher was somewhat careless.

Medical

The question of possible negligence is often linked to medical treatment or the lack of it. Under Health and Safety legislation schools must fulfil certain requirements and these will be discussed later under that heading. Apart from these the basic position is again that of the responsible parent who gives minor first aid where that is adequate but seeks professional help where there is doubt. Schools must do the same or they will be in breach of their duty of care.

Trained first aiders should be involved where possible. They will know that first aid has its limitations and that where there is doubt a doctor or an ambulance should be called.

The greatest difficulty is usually caused by situations where schools are not aware of medical conditions relating to certain pupils. When a pupil enters a school for the first time parents should be asked to record any known medical problems and advised clearly to pass on details of any later problems that may occur. If schools do this, fail to keep accurate records or check where dangerous activities are involved, and a child suffers harm then they may well be negligent. If they fail to attempt to get medical information then that may be negligent also.

Mrs Wordsworth's diary records that Jenny Duddon fainted while on a field trip. She had no record of Jenny suffering from blackouts from time to time. Perhaps the records were inaccurate or the parents had not given the information. If there had been knowledge of Jenny's blackouts should she have been allowed to go on a visit which involved hill-walking?

The onus should have been placed on the parents. Providing Mr Southey and other staff were willing, she could be allowed to go but only if her parents signed a statement accepting the risks and making it clear that in spite of these they wished her to take part. The defence of consent would then apply. Otherwise, she should not have been allowed to go – a fall on a steep hillside for someone like her could be very dangerous.

PE staff are often faced with pupils claiming excusal on that particular day, usually backed by a parental note. It is always risky to insist on participation since a good parent would not force a sick or injured child into strenuous physical effort. The teacher who insisted that a pupil with a hole-in-the-heart condition took part in a cross-country run resulting in that pupil's death provides a salutary example. Where there is a suspicion of false claims – usually forged letters – then a check should be made with parents and a medical certificate demanded if necessary. If all else fails then exclusion is the last resort.

A final problem over medical treatment for pupils is that of administering pills or medicine. Schools are under no obligation to look after these or administer them and should be wary of doing so since it could be negligent if they fell into the wrong hands or the wrong dosage was given. If consent is given then they should be kept in a locked cupboard and only during the school day.

Attendance

A question that often worries teachers is that of when their duty of care towards pupils begins and ends. Infant schools have the most difficult problem since they tend to close earlier, they are responsible for very young children and sometimes these are not collected by parents on time.

A teacher is in the place of the parent towards pupils whenever he or she is with them. This means from the time the first pupil arrives on the premises until the last one leaves and it includes all time on school visits; in the case of residential ones that means 24 hours of the day. This is a daunting task but there are some ways in which the responsibilities may be modified.

Under the law a pupil registered at a day school must attend regularly and that attendance must be recorded in a register which may be required as evidence in court proceedings and must be retained for three years after the close of the academic year. It needs to be marked carefully by a teacher (not Lucy!) and will need to show not only those present at the correct time but those who arrive late, since there is a responsibility for all pupils actually on the premises. A school needs to have some means of recording the presence of late-comers. If there is a clear record of absence then no duty of care arises. Mr Coleridges's slackness could put his school in some difficulty over the whereabouts of certain pupils.

Each school needs to make clear to parents the times of session and the earliest time at which pupils may arrive. It must arrange for some staff to be on duty from that time onwards and make it clear that no responsibility will be taken for pupils who arrive earlier. At the end of the day duty staff need to see that the premises are cleared or that pupils remaining are in the care of some responsible person.

If, in spite of this, pupils do arrive early then it is the parents who have taken a risk, though any teacher or other employee present on the premises would be in breach of their duty of care if they did not take action in an emergency. The young child frequently left at the end of a session is a more difficult problem since that child cannot be expected to go home alone. A warning to parents that responsibility will not be taken after a certain time may help and the involvement of social services or even police is possible since the parents are neglecting their children and putting them at risk. That is a desperate measure but the writer is aware of a number of heads who have been driven to take such action.

Supervision

Most of what has been said in this chapter so far is about supervision and the possible consequences if it is inadequate. There are two areas where supervision needs particular care by senior school staff.

Routine duties

Adequate supervision must be provided throughout the school day. This is especially important during breaks and before and after school – the last two often neglected by many schools. The supervision does not necessarily have to be provided by teachers, indeed they cannot be required, even in directed time, to supervise during lunch breaks.

Creating, monitoring and reviewing staff duties is the responsibility of the head. If the system is inadequate then the negligence is the head's. The teacher's responsibility is to carry out the duties as laid down, providing they are reasonable. Not to do so would be negligent on the teacher's part and would be in breach of contract. Disciplinary action could follow. Whether an injury occurs or not, Mr Coleridge is risking such action by not being with his class to mark the register and by not carrying out his patrol duties.

There is a tendency for duty systems to be created and then allowed to run for a long time without reappraisal. Organisational changes could easily mean that they have become inappropriate. Here is a series of questions to check the efficiency of your own:

1. Has the system been reviewed during the last twelve months?
2. Are the duty rotas clearly displayed?
3. Are the duties explained clearly to staff?
4. Are newly-appointed and temporary staff briefed over duties?
5. Are midday supervisors aware of their specific duties?
6. Do all staff know the action to be taken if medical attention is necessary?

7 Are all duties in directed time?

8 Are duties shared out fairly amongst staff?

9 With the safety of pupils in mind, have staff been asked for comments or suggestions?

10 Does the system take into account areas of particular difficulty such as playgrounds, corridors, toilets, car parks, bike sheds, gymnasia, laboratories, workshops, kitchens and known smoking areas and escape routes?

11 Does the system cover a short time before and after school?

12 Does a senior member of staff monitor the performance of duties?

If you are able to answer yes to all of these questions that are applicable to your school then probably you have an excellent system. It should be presented annually to the governing body – not for their approval but as evidence that it is kept under review and of concern for pupil supervision.

School visits

Most school visits pass without problems but it is in these situations where most care is needed over supervision, both for the safety of pupils and the peace of mind of those in charge, since the support of colleagues and home facilities are not available. Visits may range from a few pupils out in the immediate neighbourhood to those travelling to far-off places but the basic requirements of supervision apply to all. Although the duty to provide adequate supervision applies throughout any visit there will be times when pupils are left alone, when activities are particularly dangerous or when emergencies occur. Accidents may happen, that is acceptable. What is not acceptable is a lack of planning, a failure to guard against predictable hazards and an inadequate response to a crisis.

On the rare occasions when something does go seriously wrong a great deal of publicity is generated. This is damaging for the reputation of a school concerned, undermines the confidence of parents and causes great stress for staff. No doubt readers will remember such incidents in the Cairngorms and at Land's End but one which remains vividly in the mind and led to a panel of enquiry happened in Austria.

A party of some 45 secondary pupils and four experienced staff went up a snow-covered mountain. Warnings of the dangers were given to pupils. They were allowed to slide in safe areas but some boys chose another area of their own, although they had been warned only to use those indicated by the leaders. These boys were late in arriving back for lunch and no head count was taken – perhaps if it had some suspicions might have been aroused. In their free time after lunch some of these boys made their own way to another area of their own choosing and this proved to be particularly dangerous. Four of them slid over the edge of a precipice and died, two others managing to save themselves by hanging on to trees.

An inquiry was held. Its report said that while teachers could expect obedience and good behaviour from pupils they had to recognise the impact of exciting new surroundings and activities and the natural spirit of adventure shown by young people. In this case the staff had been complacent and the supervision was inadequate in the pupils' free time. Warnings in such a potentially dangerous situation were not enough.

Mr Southey's visit to Windermere was hardly in the same category as that to the mountain in Austria but the same considerations should have been applied. Mrs Wordsworth obtaining parental consent by telephone was somewhat risky – it could have been denied afterwards. Medical records were incomplete, although this may have been the fault of parents. If there had been knowledge of Jenny's blackouts then she might have been barred or Mr Southey could have refused to take her. If he had needed to get medical attention for her would he have known how to do so quickly?

Although each visit may raise its own peculiar issues here is a checklist that might be applicable for many visits:

- Official permission obtained
- School policies/regulations checked
- Venue checked and hazards identified
- Details sent to parents
- All activities involved stated clearly*
- Signed consent from parent/legal guardian*
- Consent form requires details of health problems
- Staffing sufficient*
- Insurance adequate*
- Away contacts for emergencies
- List of pupils with home addresses and phone numbers

- Home contacts for emergencies
- Supervision planned throughout*
- Pupils warned of potential risks
- Details recorded of accidents during visit

Those items marked * need some extra comment.

When stating the activities involved in a visit it is important to note clearly any that carry a special risk and once that has been done not to include any others, say on the spur of the moment, or parents may be able to claim they had not consented to that particular activity. If pupils are to be left unsupervised, say for shopping or individual research, then that needs to be made clear.

Schools may ask parents to sign a disclaimer, i.e. a statement that responsibility for certain matters is not accepted. To couch this in legal jargon is only likely to make parents over-anxious or even lead to a refusal to participate. No disclaimer can absolve from all responsibility but it is evidence that risks have been made clear and accepted.

Maintained schools will usually have a staff/pupil ratio laid down by the employer. Other schools will have to devise their own, preferably in consultation with the insurance company involved. The ratio will depend on the factors involved – age, activity and risk for example – but generally a ratio of 1:15 or better is necessary. Mixed parties should always include a responsible female , not necessarily a teacher.

Insurance needs some care. Maintained schools will normally be covered for local visits during school time by the LEA's policy, though these may require approval by the LEA or the governing body, the cost being met by the LEA itself or from its delegated budget to schools. Other schools will have to make their own arrangements. Such insurance usually covers negligence claims by third parties and injuries to staff, but not to pupils. This needs to be made clear to parents who can take out their own personal accident cover for their children through some such scheme as that sponsored by the National Federation of Parent Teacher Associations. This provides cover both in school and out of it.

For longer visits schools will take out a special insurance which may well include personal accident for pupils. The terms need to be checked carefully to see that they are adequate.

Overall planning of supervision for a visit may be obvious enough but if there are periods when pupils are not being directly supervised they need to be aware of where help may be obtained if needed and routine checking by staff should be arranged. Also, it is useful to remember that supervision may also be carried out on a limited basis by other adults with the party, parents or ancillary staff for example.

Further reading

A more detailed discussion of negligence will be found in any standard textbook on Law of Tort. A clear basic explanation is given in *Tort* by C. D. Baker (1991), published by Sweet and Maxwell. Supervision in relation to safety is dealt with in the DFE Safety Series which are as follows:

No 1 – *Safety in outdoor pursuits*

No 2 – *Safety in science laboratories*

No 3 – *Safety in practical studies*

No 4 – *Safety in physical education*

No 5 – *Safety at school – general advice*

10 Managing pupils – discipline, rules and sanctions

Each school needs good order and acceptable behaviour from pupils if staff are to be able to teach properly. The good order will come from efficient yet sensitive management with clear decisions taken after consultation with those affected by them and their cooperation actively sought. The acceptable behaviour will spring from that good order, from a sense of belonging, from pride in the institution, from being the object of genuine concern, from a realisation that justice is being done and from a respect for those administering it. Inevitably, even in the best of schools, there will be those who do not respond and this will often not be the fault of the schools themselves but of outside factors beyond their control. While every reasonable effort must be made to help such pupils they must not be allowed to hinder the education of others.

There must be a code of acceptable behaviour. It may be largely unwritten and if this is understood and accepted then that is good. The more that is put in writing, with all the overtones of authority, the greater the opportunities for a resentment of bureaucracy, irritation with seemingly petty regulations and hair-splitting over interpretation. As a profession teachers are far too eager to commit complicated rules to paper and fail to consider those who are on the receiving end – pupils and parents.

Some things will have to be in writing. The governing body, as part of its responsibility for a school, will need to make a general statement of policy on discipline and review this from time to time or as incidents occur. In addition, it may give directions on specific matters, for example barring the use of a certain sanction. The real responsibility, however, lies with the head.

> **'determining . . . measures to be taken with a view to promoting, among the pupils, self-discipline and proper regard for authority, encouraging good behaviour on the part of the pupils, securing that the standard of behaviour of the pupils is acceptable and otherwise regulating the conduct of the pupils; making such measures generally known within the school, and ensuring that they are implemented.'**

The *Blue Book* S.30(12)

The head, then has to decide what is the standard of behaviour that is acceptable and see that that standard is maintained. That is an enormous responsibility for one person since, in effect, he or she is the final judge in all disciplinary matters until the stage of exclusion has been reached. The need for the general support of staff, parents, governors and pupils is obvious if credibility and respect are to be maintained.

The framework for discipline in a school will be the rules. Responsibility for their creation and observance lies with the head.

Rules

There are grounds for saying that the head's power to make the rules has legal force. Maintained schools are controlled by Parliament through the Education Acts and the DFE which issues the conditions of service, thus giving the head responsibility for making rules. So by a somewhat lengthy chain there is statutory authority. The head's powers are also supported by case law where in a number of instances judges have stated that someone must be responsible for discipline and the making of rules and that person is the head.

If the head seems to have limitless power to make decisions over school rules we have to ask if those powers may be challenged. The answer is yes. In the first place, they may be in breach of the general policy laid down by the governors or of specific instructions given by them. In the second place, they may be in breach of instructions which an LEA is entitled to give, though these are fast-diminishing with the introduction of LMS. They may even be challenged under the criminal law (e.g. a rule which is in breach of Health and Safety legislation) or under the law relating to discrimination (remember the boy Sikh and his turban). Lastly, they may be challenged on grounds of unreasonableness by an approach to the governing body which is then able to give a specific instruction to the head if it wishes to do so. However, it would be difficult to challenge rules drawn up after consultation and which were based on a clear concern for good order and the safety and welfare of pupils and staff generally.

Unless rules can be challenged on any of the grounds stated then pupils must obey them and courts have held that reasonable cooperation from parents may be expected. It is important, then, for parents to be told of rules that exist. Some will be obvious, such as a requirement for good behaviour and obedience in class, but others may not, for example those for pupils leaving a school during school sessions, rules concerning pupils on school visits or those relating to punishments. These need to be communicated to the parents of each child entering a school for the first time, or earlier if possible, probably in the prospectus now required by law.

A parent who objects to such rules now, under the principle of open enrolment, may seek a place elsewhere. The parent of a current pupil who objects to a known and reasonable rule may seek a transfer. Of course, communication of rules has a drawback – a parent can allege that a school is not enforcing the rules that it has made and that is all the more reason for considering their content very carefully.

Parents who would otherwise support school rules sometimes object to their enforcement for incidents that take place off the premises. Commonsense dictates that when teachers are in charge of outside visits the rules apply, since those staff are *in loco parentis* throughout. The objections come when pupils are disciplined for misbehaviour on the way to or from school. It is true that once pupils reach a school's boundaries at the recognised end of a session responsibility may cease and no action be taken. However, most schools are sensitive over their reputation locally and wish to control behaviour to some extent when pupils are on the way to or from school, as well as prevent bullying and conduct that could be dangerous on streets and buses. Case law supports the right of schools to make rules covering such situations.

Cleary v Booth 1893 concerned two boys who were punished for fighting on the way to school. The judge upheld the right to take this action and apply rules to behaviour outside school hours and off the premises:

'Can it reasonably be argued that the only right of a schoolmaster to inflict punishment is in respect of acts done in school . . . It is difficult to express in words the extent of the schoolmaster's authority in respect to the punishment of his pupils; but in my opinion his authority extends, not only to acts done in school, but also to cases where a complaint of actions done out of school, at any rate while going to and from school, is made to the schoolmaster.

A much later case in Shropshire upheld the right to punish a pupil for breaking a rule by smoking in the street outside school, even though the father alleged that his consent had been given. It can be stated with confidence that school rules may be applied when pupils are on the way to or from school and should be applied during all school visits and sports fixtures. This needs to be made clear to both pupils and parents.

Appearance

The most damaging confrontations over school rules usually seem to concern appearance and dress. The head has the power to decide what is acceptable but, except in independent schools, there can be no requirement for a particular school uniform. So the head may ban jeans, combat jackets, studded belts, jewellery, peculiar hair styles or the various trappings of current fashion – many of these on grounds of safety alone. As the law stands – and, in view of the new delegated powers, a test case might decide differently – uniform cannot be insisted upon.

The evidence from cases that have reached the courts is that in a disagreement the head is likely to win but at the expense of considerable argument, media attention and stress. Many of such struggles seem futile and could have been avoided with some flexibility shown by both sides. Today, a dissatisfied parent may always seek a place at another school.

A good example of commonsense prevailing comes from a recent incident at a girls' school near Manchester. The rule was that girls could not wear trousers and this had become an issue between the head and the parents of Asian girls, where the tradition was that trousers should be worn. The details were seized upon by the press but before a major incident was created the head and governors reconsidered the rule and agreed to change it, provided that the trousers were in the colour appropriate to the uniform and this was happily accepted by both sides.

Discrimination

The law relating to discrimination applies to pupils as well as to staff. In Birmingham it was held to be discrimination by the LEA when it provided fewer places for girls than boys at its grammar schools. To promote boys from one class to another rather than girls has been held to constitute discrimination. It would be discriminatory to close certain subjects to either boys or girls.

If the Manchester school had been a mixed one then banning trousers for girls might well have amounted to discrimination, as might the banning of earrings for boys when girls are allowed to wear them.

Times and attitudes change and while consistency over rules is important so is review and flexibility.

Review

Imagine that you have the task of re-assessing your own rules. They have been in existence for some time and are now to be reproduced in the prospectus which, by law, you are required to provide for parents. Here are some questions to ask in reaching conclusions over their relevance and efficiency:

1. Can the rules be justified on the need for good behaviour, order and safety?
2. Are they expressed in plain language so that all may understand?
3. A long list of 'shalt nots' is forbidding to many and challenging to some. Are the rules expressed positively where possible and not negatively?
4. Rules that cannot be enforced are pointless. Are all yours reasonable in that sense? Be particularly careful over dress.
5. Is a clear ban placed on smoking, alcohol, knives, fireworks, matches, lighters, electrical equipment and any other items considered to be particularly dangerous?
6. Are the rules clear over time of arrival at school, time of leaving and procedure to be followed if leaving during a session? Have breaks and lunch-times been included? Are there clear ways of explaining absence?
7. Do the rules cover known trouble spots on site? Are 'no-go areas' clearly stated?
8. Are instructions given as to action to be taken in case of illness, accident or the outbreak of fire?
9. Is there a clear policy for pupils asking to bring bicycles or even cars onto the premises?
10. There may be local hazards such as busy roads, dangerous exits or nearby industrial sites. Have these been accounted for?
11. Do the rules avoid discrimination?
12. The rules need to be made clear to pupils, staff and parents. How is this to be achieved?

Once the rules have been drafted there needs to be consultation. Others will spot errors and possible omissions. The consultation should not be limited to staff since parents, who will have to deal with the inevitable arguments at home, will often have useful suggestions and so may pupils, who will be acutely aware of the impact of the rules during the daily round. The head is responsible for the final decisions.

Sanctions

Any code of discipline will entail sanctions against those who are in breach of it. Good teachers will try to deal with disciplinary problems without recourse to formal sanctions but at times they will have to be used. When this happens the sanctions should be those known and accepted by parents, pupils and staff. Bizarre punishments devised by certain individuals only illustrate a lack of professional responsibility and judgment.

Teachers are in the same basic position as parents. Parents have authority under the law to punish their children in a reasonable way. They still have one right that teachers do not – that of administering reasonable corporal punishment. On the other hand, parents cannot decline responsibility for their children – schools may do so through the exclusion process.

Teachers, then, may discipline pupils in most ways that a responsible parent might use. Apart from the use of obvious punishments such as extra work, internal chores or the withdrawal of privileges, there are some sanctions where the legal basis may be difficult to interpret and two where there are specific problems because of developments in the law.

Detention

To restrict the liberty of another without legal right is the form of trespass to the person known as false imprisonment. One defence to such is that of parental authority and, as parent substitutes, this is the defence that teachers could put forward over the detention of pupils. However, a teacher is *in loco parentis* temporarily. Children do not have to attend school – they may be educated 'otherwise', as the 1944 Act puts it – so a parent has a right to withdraw his child at any time from a teacher's authority.

In one case heard in a Lancashire county court the judge held that detention for a short time after school was a lawful punishment but, as the case went no further, there is no binding precedent on the matter.

Detention during morning and afternoon breaks raises no problems and the teacher restricts the liberty of the child just as a parent might. Detention at lunch-time is certainly possible for those remaining for a meal on site. Detention after school seems to be permissible but is very risky for younger pupils and there is a particular problem where pupils are entitled to free transport home. If they are kept in and left behind by buses then a right to the free ride still exists.

All in all, detention after school hardly seems worthwhile. If a school uses it then parents need to be told that it is a recognised sanction, warning should be given beforehand and there should be a time limit set. Of course, supervision has to be provided.

Confiscation

Whether it can be described as a sanction or a measure of safety, confiscation raises problems for teachers. A responsible parent might remove articles from a child as a punishment or on grounds of safety and so may teachers. However, once items have been confiscated then responsibility has to be taken for them. In his time the writer has confiscated cigarettes, matches, lighters, razor blades, bayonets, flick knives, knuckle dusters, valuable jewellery, condoms, a shotgun, a magazine of live tommy-gun ammunition and a brace of ferrets, amongst other items. If due care had not been taken over their keeping and security, they had been lost or stolen or someone had been injured (bitten by an escaped ferret, say!) then negligence could have been alleged.

Unfortunately, not to confiscate could be negligent if there is a real risk and teachers do nothing. Parents need to be told that articles banned under the rules and others creating dangers will be confiscated. When this happens a letter should be sent home asking them to collect the offending item and pointing out that if this does not happen after a reasonable time the property will be destroyed. Under the Local Government (Miscellaneous Provisions) Act of 1982 S.41 there is a right to destroy or dispose of unclaimed or lost property. Items such as live ammunition, those amounting to offensive weapons or arousing suspicion of drugs should be handed to the police, whose advice should be sought if there is any doubt.

Teachers should not say that confiscated items will never be returned, for that comes close to the definition of theft – the dishonest taking of the property of another with the intention of keeping it permanently. Confiscated items should not be used for a teacher's own purposes, that certainly constitutes theft.

Physical force

The use of physical force against another is a form of trespass to the person. It usually consists of an assault – a threat of violence causing fear – and a battery – the actual application of the unlawful force. Both assault and battery may amount to criminal acts so one particular incident may lead to a prosecution and/or a suit for civil damages. The criminal hearing takes precedence. Strictly speaking, a parent who spanks a naughty child commits the criminal act and the trespass but the defence of parental authority applies. Parents who go beyond what is reasonable should be prosecuted.

Many teachers feel that, because of changes in the law regarding corporal punishment, the defence of parental authority no longer applies to them, even though they are acting as parent substitutes. This is only partly true.

Corporal punishment was a traditional sanction used in British schools. Most of it – the box on the ear or the slipper on the backside – was always illegal and, indeed, dangerous. Few objections were raised, presumably because parents expected it, had experienced it at school themselves or used similar methods at home. In schools maintained by LEAs the only corporal punishment that was legal was that authorised by the local regulations. These usually stipulated by whom the punishment was to be given and by which method – usually the cane. Details had to be recorded in a punishment book, which was open to inspection by HMI and the governors. In other schools the position was vague though the right to use corporal punishment under delegated parental authority was recognised. Independent schools may still use it.

Investigation into the conduct of several schools during the '60s and '70s revealed the extent of beating that was being used and public anxiety over such treatment increased. In Scotland, corporal punishment was traditionally administered by use of the tawse, a leather strap. Two Scottish ladies, Mrs Campbell and Mrs Cosans, decided to require that it should not be used on their children. The head would not agree and eventually the case reached the European Court of Human Rights in 1982.

Britain was a signatory to the Convention for the Protection of Human Rights and Fundamental Freedoms, as a result of which agreement the Court of Human Rights was established – not to be confused with the European Court of Justice of the European Community. The agreed provisions have not yet been assimilated into the laws of the U.K. but they exert great influence over the interpretation of national legislation.

Corporal punishment was challenged on the grounds that it constituted inhumane and degrading treatment. The Court did not declare that corporal punishment should be banned but decided, in effect, that it was an infringement of parental rights and parents should be allowed to opt out of such treatment for their children if they wished. The U.K. response was to attempt to introduce a Bill allowing parents to exercise such choice. This was manifestly absurd since in schools some pupils would be subject to corporal punishment and others would not.

Fortunately, the Bill was lost. Finally, as part of the Education (No 2) Act 1986 corporal punishment was banned in state schools and this came into force in August 1987.

The Act, however, does not preclude the use of physical force by teachers. S.46 makes it clear that force may be used to prevent personal injury to the child, other pupils, teachers or anyone else. Force may also be used to protect property. This puts teachers in the position of parents who may have to use force to prevent injuries, stop fighting or prevent damage. Of course, force used in any of these circumstances must be reasonable.

Mrs Wordsworth in her diary recorded Michael Shepherd's allegation that Miss Dove had slapped him in the face. If this turned out to be true what might happen? Teachers may lose control, just as parents may do.

Mrs Wordsworth needs to establish what really occurred – if anything did – but her diary does not suggest any obvious physical harm. If there has been a slap, what follows will depend upon the attitude of the parents. If they are the really old-fashioned sort then Michael might receive another slap; if they appreciate the stress to Miss Dove by Michael's conduct they might express their disapproval but let the matter rest there; they might decide to take things further because they believe Michael incapable of bad behaviour – he is so good at home, because of a desire to make life difficult for Miss Dove or, indeed, as a matter of principle.

They might complain to the head, who could consider disciplinary action, especially if there have been previous incidents of a similar nature involving Miss Dove. They might submit a written complaint to the governors who should then ask the head to investigate. The first would be the most sensible course. They might decide to go law.

Technically, as we saw earlier, what has happened constitutes assault and battery and this may be criminal or civil. The Shepherds may go to the police who must investigate but, unless there is some evidence of actual bodily injury, a prosecution is most unlikely. The Shepherds may bring a private prosecution but they will have to bear the cost themselves and they are unlikely to succeed. They could sue for damages in a civil court but, even if successful, would be likely to obtain only nominal damages and be left with their own costs to pay. Unless they were pursuing some sort of vendetta then it would hardly be worthwhile.

All this should not hide the distress caused to Miss Dove by threats of legal action. She needs advice and support from senior staff in dealing with difficult pupils. If she loses control again and some injury occurs – say a cut from a ring on her finger – then a prosecution is much more likely.

Exclusion

Mrs Wordsworth's diary also reveals problems with a very difficult pupil – Alice Fell. She disrupts lessons, fights with other pupils and has threatened them with a knife. Presumably, other disciplinary measures have been tried without success and Mrs Wordsworth has been unable to gain the cooperation of the parents. In order to maintain discipline and safety drastic action needs to be taken and this means exclusion.

Before the passing of the Education (No 2) Act of 1986 terms such as suspension, exclusion and expulsion were used loosely and had different meanings in different areas. For example, some LEAs delegated power to heads to exclude, others did not. Some involved governors, others did not. The Act attempts to set out a recognised procedure to be followed by all state schools, with some minor variations, when dealing with exclusions but the result '. . . reflects the niceties of the parliamentary draftsman rather than a straightforward way of dealing quickly but fairly with the issues'. It makes a great deal of work for any school involved but certainly persistently disruptive pupils may now be dealt with. The result has been an increasing number of permanent exclusions, thus creating a headache for LEAs who still have the responsibility under the 1944 Act of providing education for all.

The requirements for exclusion, the only term now to be used, are to be found in Ss. 22–27 of the 1986 Act. We can apply them to Alice's case.

Only the head, or the deputy acting as head, may exclude. This may be for up to five days in any one term and the head is under no obligation to inform the LEA or the governors though it should certainly be included in the next report to them. If the exclusion would entail the pupils missing a public examination then it must be reported, even if it is for one day only. So Alice may be excluded for a short period but the head is obliged, without delay, to inform her parents of the reasons for it and explain their right to make representations to the governors and the LEA.

The head might have decided to exclude Alice for a period longer than five days or for an indefinite period – perhaps until her parents attend to have proper discussions. If so, the governors and the LEA must be informed and parents given reasons for the exclusion and details of their right of appeal. In such cases the governors may direct the head to re-admit Alice before the fixed period is up or order the indefinite period to be terminated, either immediately or at some future date. The head must comply. If the LEA orders re-admittance then the head may block this by making the exclusion permanent.

Perhaps the temporary exclusion brings Alice's parents to school and they and the staff together try to overcome the problems but Alice remains intractable and continues to be a serious threat to discipline and the safety of others. The result will have to be permanent exclusion. We are now entering an even more complicated area, though a similar procedure has to be followed over parental rights.

The governors may order re-admittance or uphold the decision of the head (the head alone has no power to re-admit). The governors must provide for parents to be able to appeal against the decision if it goes against them. The LEA must be informed and, after consulting with the governors, must make its own decision. Both parents and governors must be able to appeal against that decision. In voluntary aided and special agreement schools the governors decide but must make provision for parental appeal. Grant maintained schools have the same responsibility.

Appeals against an LEA decision go to a special independent panel which each LEA must set up – usually the same one that deals with appeals over school admissions. Even the Secretary of State has no power to overrule this panel unless it can be shown to be acting illegally. The only other course open is a referral to the local Ombudsman, who has power to investigate procedures but not to change decisions.

When a pupil reaches the age of 18 the above provisions apply to him or her and not to parents, who have then no legal rights over exclusion.

Mr and Mrs Fell, Alice, the head and governors may have been caught up in this complicated situation, which may be even more complex. The Articles of Government for a particular school may contain variations on what has been described and this is permissible within the framework of the Act.

If permanent exclusion is upheld, what happens to Alice? She may be given a chance to make a fresh start at another school, if there is one with a vacant place. She may attend a special unit set up by the LEA, given a place at a special residential school or provided with the inadequate and desperate remedy of home tuition. Responsibility lies with the LEA.

Here are some points for heads and senior staff to bear in mind when caught up in the complexities of exclusion:

1. Be aware of the particular provisions for exclusions in your own Articles of Government and see that these are followed to the letter.

2. Unless the situation is really serious do not exclude until other methods of solving the problem have been tried and parents and outside agencies have been involved. Keep records of these.

3. Only exclude after calm consideration. Beware of hasty decisions which may be hard to justify later.

4 Wherever possible, use a short or indefinite exclusion first. This shows a willingness to try to solve the problem. Permanent exclusion may always be used later.

5 Ensure that the reasons for exclusion are plain and that the evidence is to hand so that this may be shown to parents and, if necessary, to governors and the LEA.

6 Throughout an exclusion process ensure that parents are told of their rights.

7 If you have a good case and the pupil concerned is a real threat in some way to other pupils or to staff you can expect support from governors and appeal committees. However, they have a duty to see that your action has been fair. If your action is arbitrary, your case ill-prepared or the rights of others ignored you may be overruled.

Test yourself

1 When Tommy Atkins comes to school his teachers are substitutes for his parents. Does this mean that they must act as Mr and Mrs Atkins would do?

2 It is a frosty morning and the playground is icy. Pupils have made a slide and are enjoying themselves. The member of staff on patrol has seen the sliding and has allowed it to continue but Richard falls awkwardly and sustains a serious fracture. His parents contemplate an action for negligence. What must they prove?

3 One defence to a negligence action is that of consent. How might this apply in school situations?

4 While children are in school they do not have to be supervised continuously. How far is this true?

5 To what extent are pupils covered by insurance if they are injured during school activities?

6 Are there any legal requirements as to the ratio of staff to pupils?

7 'You must not punish Arthur for what he has done outside school. It's none of your business.' Thus wrote Mrs F. Was she right?

8 In what circumstances may teachers use physical force against pupils?

9 Before a PE lesson a number of girls handed watches to the teacher for safe keeping. At the end of the lesson Mary was slow to change and when she went to collect her watch there were none left. What are the consequences for the teacher?

10 Only the head may exclude a pupil. Who may authorise re-admission?

Comments will be found at the end of the book (on page 203).

11 The school and parents

Amanda Toogood

Amanda is a Year 9 pupil at the Faraway High School and has been there for about six months. She is a pupil of average ability, pleasant enough but giving the impression of being rather spoilt. Often her homework is late or incomplete but there are always explanations from her parents. Frequently, she is excused from PE lessons because of colds, onset of periods or headaches – all supported by letters from her mother. Her attendance is erratic but not enough to warrant action.

Mrs Toogood has visited school to see form teacher, year tutor and other senior staff on various matters – all involving complaints concerning Amanda's treatment at school. Mr Toogood has made no contact until today.

He and his wife arrive and ask to see the head. They have no appointment. They stand waiting for some ten minutes or so and then a secretary tells them that this is not possible but an appointment could be made for the following day. Possibly they could see a deputy if they could wait for half an hour. At this, Mr Toogood loses his temper and shouts that only the man at the top will do and that he will find the head's office himself.

As the shouting increases and there are interested witnesses present the secretary becomes alarmed and contacts the head on the intercom. He sends away the member of staff with whom he is conferring, comes to the reception area and attempts to calm the Toogoods by taking them to his office. It takes some time to persuade Mr Toogood even to sit down.

Once some kind of order has been restored the head asks the parents to explain the reasons for their visit. Mr Toogood does the talking and his wife merely nods her head at intervals. Amanda is being bullied by other pupils, victimised by staff and not being taught properly. No information reaches parents. There is no evidence of Amanda's work or standard of performance. She is made to take subjects which she does not like such as sex education, PE and RE. The school rules are silly. His wife has not been listened to when she has visited school. The staff are incompetent and the head himself is living in cloud-cuckoo-land if he thinks all is well. If he, Mr Toogood, ran his business in such a way he would soon be bankrupt.

The school has a good reputation locally and the head is proud of it. He is stung by the criticisms, Mr Toogood's lack of courtesy and the wild accusations. He responds angrily, defending his staff and his organisation and methods.

The atmosphere becomes even more heated. Eventually, Mr Toogood jumps to his feet declaring that he will take Amanda away and will make complaints to the governors, the Chief Education Officer and his MP. Followed by his wife, he storms out and slams the door violently behind him.

Readers will know that during the course of a school year they can expect, to a greater or lesser extent, confrontations of a similar kind. They provide some of the most daunting tests of a school's ability to manage relationships with parents. Sometimes, of course, there will be failure but with sensitive planning, efficient organisation and communication and a readiness to review arrangements the chance of success may be greatly increased.

Test Yourself

Look again at this incident and give your own answers to the following questions:

1 Do the Toogoods have a case? What are their rights over the issues they raise?

2 What is your assessment of the handling of the situation by the head and other staff?

3 If there are any lessons to be learned here, what are they?

See the end of the book (p 206) for the writer's comments and compare them with your own.

Parental rights

Parents have both rights and responsibilities with regard to their children. The main responsibility that concerns us here is that laid down in the Education Act 1944 S.36:

'It shall be the duty of the parent of every child of compulsory school age to cause him to receive efficient full-time education suitable to his age, ability and aptitude, [and to any special educational needs he may have] either by regular attendance at school or otherwise.'

Failure to meet with that responsibility may lead to prosecution and even to a child being removed from the parents under care proceedings. All this does not mean that a child has to attend a school but that an education must be provided somehow. If the child is educated by attendance at school then that attendance must be regular and it is accompanied by a number of rights. These relate to the following:

Information

Choice of school

Curriculum

Special needs

Reports

RE and assemblies

Consultation

Election of parent governors

Annual parents' meeting

Opting out

Complaints and appeals

Information

Of all the rights extended to parents this is perhaps the most significant. Previously, basic information relating to a school's organisation and even details of a pupil's performance were given to parents only by grace and favour. Parents could remain ignorant of a school's structures, its routines, discipline and syllabuses of work. They could be denied reports and consultation, as indeed happened during the industrial troubles of the 'eighties. Of course, many schools did give information to parents but there was no obligation to do so.

Now parents are entitled by law to a great deal of information. LEAs must produce general information for their areas but details for each school are the responsibility of governors though the LEA publishes them.

Aided and special agreement schools must publish them themselves. Details of the information to be provided are given in the following:

- Education (School Information) Regulations 1981
- Education (School Curriculum and Related Information) Regulations 1989
- Education (School Hours and Policies Information) Regulations 1989
- Education (Information on School Examination Results) (England) Regulations 1991
- DFE Circulars 14/89 and 9/91 give guidance

The amount of information required is considerable – far too much to list here – and it ranges from the name of the head and chair of governors through to full details of examination results. Several provisions need some special mention. Schemes of work and syllabuses must be available for parents to see, along with any communication from the DEF relating to the National Curriculum. Details of the nature of religious education given must be available and so must copies of any reports made by HMI. Finally, there must be information as to how complaints may be made relating to the curriculum.

Parents are now entitled to receive the information in the form of a single prospectus and not by separate sheets or letters. Independent schools need to remember that since they are offering services in return for payment their prospectuses are covered by the Trade Descriptions Act, a breach of which can lead to a criminal prosecution.

Choice of school

There is really nothing new in the right of parents to choose a particular school. S.76 of the 1944 Act states that, 'pupils are to be educated in accordance with the wishes of their parents'. This is qualified by, 'as far as is compatible with the provision of efficient instruction and training and the avoidance of unreasonable public expenditure'.

This is reinforced in S.6 of the 1980 Act which requires compliance with parental choice of school unless this would, 'prejudice the provision of efficient education or the efficient use of resources'.

These provisions, together with the 1986 and 1988 Acts, mean that parents have a free choice of school. In Cleveland a recent clash between the right to choice and possible discrimination on grounds of race ended with the court declaring that parental choice was an absolute right, whatever the reasons for it. However, there are limitations on that choice. The most obvious one is that of a school's standard number. If a school is below its standard number then it cannot refuse a place to a parent who applies unless it is still a selective school or where, as in the case of Aided or Special Agreement schools, there is an agreed arrangement between governors and the LEA over admission criteria – for example on grounds of religion.

Calculation of the standard admission number is complicated. In the case of secondary schools it is the number taken in during 1979–80 or 1989–90 if that is higher. If a school opened after 1979 then its standard number will have been fixed at the opening. The number applies to age groups so a school could be up to its number in one age group but below it in another, thus causing problems where parents wish to transfer several children to a particular school at the same time. Without going through a complicated procedure it is not possible to lower a standard admission number but it is relatively easy to raise it, the main criterion being physical capacity as defined by the DFE.

Regulations for standard admission numbers will be found in Ss. 26–32 of the 1986 (No 2) Act and special arrangements for primary schools in the SI Education (Variation of Standard Numbers for Primary Schools) Order 1991.

A less obvious restriction on parental choice is that of transport. Free transport must be provided for pupils under eight and living over two miles beyond their school and for pupils over eight who live more than three miles away. This only applies to pupils living within the particular catchment area. If a parent opts for a school outside that area then there is no entitlement to free transport.

Exercise of parental choice, then, may well depend upon conditions in a particular area or the relative affluence of parents. It also means that parents at odds with a school may find a place elsewhere more easily than before.

Curriculum

The requirement of the 1944 Act that schools must provide efficient education suitable to a child's age, ability and aptitude still applies but is now augmented by the responsibility to consider special educational needs and to implement the National Curriculum.

LEAs must issue a statement of curriculum policy. Governors must consider this and may modify it if they wish but, if they do so, must notify the LEA. The governors then issue their own statement which is given to the head to implement in detail. It must comply with the

National Curriculum but may contain other matters. Two are of particular concern.

The first is that of religious education and arrangements for assemblies. Religious education is not part of the National Curriculum but it is a requirement for all state schools. In county and controlled schools it must follow a syllabus agreed by the local SACRE (Standing Advisory Council for Religious Education) and this must be non-denominational. It must be mainly Christian in approach but with due regard for other faiths. In aided and special agreement schools governors decide on the syllabus in accordance with their deed of trust. Grant maintained schools follow the agreed syllabus or make their own proposals, which are subject to approval by the Secretary of State.

Religious education does not have to be provided as a separate subject and parents have two rights concerning it. They may withdraw their children from it or insist that it be given in accordance with the agreed syllabus or the terms of the trust deed, if this is applicable.

Parents also have a right to withdraw their children from the daily act of worship which the law requires schools to hold. This no longer has to be held at the beginning of the day and it may consist of one large assembly or a number of smaller ones. The majority, but not all, of the assemblies must be of a broadly Christian character but not denominational. The SACRE has power in exceptional circumstance to excuse a school, or a section of it, from this requirement.

The DFE Circular: *Religious Education and Collective Worship* gives advice on these matters.

The second item of concern is sex education. It is entirely a matter for the governors as to whether this should be part of the curriculum or not and their policy in the matter must be stated. If they decide to include it then it must show due regard for morals and family life and it becomes a compulsory element of the curriculum unless governors decide to allow opting out. Heads will be interested to know that if the governors' policy is incompatible with a syllabus for an external examination then they are not bound to follow it in that area of the curriculum.

Again there is an advisory DFE Circular: *Sex Education at School*.

Special needs

Good schools have always tried to give help to pupils with special problems but there was little in legislation before 1981 that made such help mandatory. Largely as a result of the Warnock Report, the Education Act 1981 was passed. This requires LEAs, governors and heads to make provision for children who come into the defined category.

A pupil has special educational needs if he or she has a learning difficulty greater than that experienced by the majority of children of that age or there is an obvious physical handicap. An attempt to persuade a court that under the Act gifted children qualify for special help failed. There must be a blockage or hindrance to learning of some kind, though what constitutes a 'difficulty' is open to interpretation.

Pupils with special educational needs fall into two categories. One, the more serious, is where a pupil is 'statemented' by the LEA and this process will probably involve experts such as doctors and psychologists. If a statement is made then it must indicate clearly the need recognised and the help that is to be provided. The responsibility for that help lies with the LEA. In 1987 the Court of Appeal ruled that an LEA has some discretion as to whether a statement should be made and a more recent case has decided that if a statement is made then it must cover all the child's needs and not just certain aspects.

The other category of pupils, those with less serious difficulties, are also entitled to help but that must be provided within a school's normal resources and failure to do so may lead to a complaint to governors.

The governors are responsible for designating someone to be responsible in their school for the oversight of the provision of help for pupils with special educational needs. This may well be the head but it could be a governor and in larger schools it could be members of staff.

Many pupils with learning difficulties will not be able to cope with the full demands of the National Curriculum. The head may excuse them from all or part of it but parents must be consulted and they have a right of appeal to governors over the head's decision. In any case, the head must review any such excusal at six-monthly intervals.

Reports and consultation

Parents are not only entitled to general information regarding their child's school but also particular information regarding that child's progress and a chance to discuss it with teachers. Most schools would do this anyway and most would exceed what the law requires.

Under the Education (Individual Pupils' Achievements) (Information) Regulations 1990 all state schools must produce by 31st July each year an annual report to the parents of each child giving, in particular, details of performance under the National Curriculum and statutory tests and details of other subjects and activities, though these are not specified. If a pupil is exempted from all or part of the National Curriculum then this must be made clear in the report.

The legal requirements are thus basic and most schools would consider them inadequate if good relationships with parents are to be maintained. The DFE issues a Circular: *Records of Achievement* which gives further advice more in keeping with good practice in schools but this is not mandatory. It does, in addition, set out a useful framework for the pupil profiles that many schools have developed. These record a pupil's achievements and interests and become his or her property on leaving school. They provide useful information for prospective employers as well as a souvenir of a school career.

As we shall see shortly, parents have a right to complain or appeal on a number of issues but the right to consultation is very limited. Most schools encourage it and the head has power to direct staff to consult with parents during directed time. However, if the head were to insist that a teacher met an aggressive or particularly difficult parent that could well amount to an unreasonable instruction. The degree of consultation therefore is very much a matter for each school and parental rights are restricted to the provision of information already mentioned.

Parent governors

Until the impact of recent legislation governors were somewhat shadowy figures with little real power. Parents, and indeed some teachers, did not even know who their governors were and their method of appointment was something of a mystery. They were not appointed by parents and were not accountable to them. Legislation has changed both these aspects.

Earlier, we saw that parents are entitled to elect one element of the governing body. Responsibility for conducting the election lies with the LEA or, in the case of aided, special agreement and grant maintained schools with the governors, but arrangements are usually delegated to the head. Whoever is responsible must see that all reasonable efforts are made to inform parents of the vacancies, that candidates are eligible as parents of pupils and are proposed and seconded by others similarly qualified, that the method of election is clearly explained to parents and that the results are communicated to them. The ballot must be a secret one.

The statutory provisions are to be found in S.15 of the Education (No 2) Act 1986 and advice over the holding of elections is given in DFE Circular 7/87. The number of parent governors and their terms of office will be found in each school's Articles of Government.

Parent governors sit as individuals and are not subject to mandate from any body such as a PTA but they have an obvious responsibility to reflect the general views of parents if these are known.

Parents have a right for their governors to hold an annual parents' meeting. This is a meeting where the governors, not the head alone, have to account for their running of the school. It must be held annually and the parents of all registered pupils given a chance to attend.

The governors are required by S.30 of the 1986 Act to produce a report which summarises how they have discharged their duties during the preceding year. The contents and style are left to them but advice will be found in another DFE Circular of 8/86 and the emphasis should be on simple reporting that is clear to parents. The report must be sent to all parents and the object of the meeting is for them to discuss it and to raise any other matters. When at least 50% of the pupils are boarders the governors must produce a report but need not hold a meeting.

There is no quorum for such a meeting and it must go ahead even if only one parent attends. For a formal resolution to be passed parents present must be at least equal to 20% of the number of pupils on roll and any such resolution carried must be considered later by the governors and commented upon in their next annual report. No doubt, governors would take note of any comments made even if no formal resolution could be taken.

In many schools the annual parents' meeting is very poorly attended and has become something of a joke with teachers. This is a pity since it does give parents a chance to see and hear their governors and give them some criticisms to consider. Perhaps it is most likely to succeed if combined with some other school function.

Appeals and complaints

Today, parents have rights of making appeals and complaints in a number of ways and over a range of issues. They should always be encouraged to bring an internal complaint to the head in the first place since, if the matter can be settled at that level, it will bring a speedy solution which will be of benefit to all sides and will avoid the inevitable stress and effort entailed in the bureaucratic entanglements that will otherwise follow.

We have seen already that parents may complain to governors over various matters and may appeal to them formally over exclusions. We have seen that parents may make final appeals to independent panels over admissions and exclusions. There are other possibilities.

There has always been a right of appeal to the Secretary of State under S.68 or S.99 of the 1944 Act on the grounds that an LEA or governing body is acting unreasonably or failing to carry out its duties. This has always been a daunting prospect for parents and, while it is still open to them as a last resort, the Education Reform Act 1988 under S.23 attempts to make arrangements for complaints to be dealt with at local level.

The requirement now is for LEAs to make arrangements for parents to complain on matters relating to the curriculum where they believe the LEA or the governors are acting unreasonably. The Act does not spell out the matters to be covered but DFE Circular: *Local Arrangements for the Consideration of Complaints* mentions the National Curriculum, RE and religious assemblies, external examinations, information over the curriculum and charging policies. Other matters could be included under the general terms of S.23.

The parent must be able to complain in person and may be accompanied by an adviser or interpreter, if so desired. The means of contact must be made clear and both LEA and governors involved, but not the head. If agreement cannot be reached then the complaint goes to the Secretary of State.

These arrangements do not apply to complaints against the LEA over the statementing of a child with special educational needs. Here, under S.8 of the 1981 Act, parents have a right to appeal to a local appeals committee which the LEA must set up and under S.5 of the same Act a right of appeal to the Secretary of State. Finally, parents might go to the High Court alleging that the LEA is not performing its statutory duty. This process is known as judicial review and the court may order the LEA to perform its duty under the Act. Judicial review should only be sought when other approaches have failed and it is not in the nature of an appeal against a decision but is an allegation that there is a legal flaw in what has taken place.

Attendance

Modern legislation has extended parental rights with regard to the education of their children but it has not diminished their responsibilities. Earlier in this chapter we mentioned the basic responsibility of parents under the 1944 Act to see that their children are educated, 'either by regular attendance at school or otherwise'. The 'otherwise' may be satisfied by teaching given at home by parents or private tutors but such tuition is open to inspection by the local LEA. Where it is inadequate parents may be prosecuted and, in extreme cases, children even taken into care. The 1988 Act makes no provision for pupils being educated 'otherwise' but since the National Curriculum is not mandatory for pupils in independent schools it could hardly be applied to those being educated at home.

Schools must maintain an admission register and this may now be computerised. The latest legal requirements are to be found in the SI Education (Pupils' Attendance Records) 1991. The details must include the full name, sex, exact date of birth and of admission and the name and address of any last school. It must record the name and address of any known parent of a child and, against the name of any parent having responsibility, a telephone number for contact if that is possible. If a child is a boarder then this must be indicated.

If there is any doubt over age then a school may ask to see a birth certificate. If parents refuse then a copy may be obtained for a fee by a school since registration of births, deaths or marriages is open to public inspection.

Schools must maintain attendance registers and these must be kept for at least three years after the end of the school year in which they have been used. They are open to inspection by HMI and other authorised persons. Since they are legal documents which may be required as evidence in the prosecution of parents or applications for education supervision orders their careful maintenance is of importance. They are also important for checking the physical presence of pupils because of the need for adequate supervision, handling of emergencies and monitoring attendance.

Again, the recent legislation is in the SI of 1991, which amends earlier legislation of 1956, 1988 and 1989. DFE Circular 11/91 gives guidelines on the interpretation of the legislation. The main purpose seems to be to force schools to publish attendance and truancy rates in the prospectus for parents required by law. However, it does also clarify arrangements over attendance in various ways, the 1956 regulations being somewhat vague. That legislation only required the recording of presence or absence. The new rules go much further.

Registers must be marked in ink at the beginning of morning and afternoon sessions and attendance may be computerised. The registers must show the difference between authorised and unauthorised absence so that truancy rates may be calculated. The actual format of registers is a local matter but uniformity for an LEA's schools is stressed in order to assist the work of welfare staff. Likewise, the method of recording absence is for local decision but a suggested code is given in the Circular as a means of establishing which absence is authorised and which is not. This is as follows:

B Receiving part-time or temporary education off-site

C Other circumstances (specified)

E Exclusion for a fixed or indefinite period

H Annual family holiday (permission granted)

I Attending interview

M Medical/dental

P Approved sporting activity

R Day of religious observance

S Study leave

V Educational visit

W Work experience

O Late (after registration closed)

The lateness of pupils presents a particular problem for schools. It is well established by case law in *Hinchley v Rankin 1961* that a pupil who arrives after the register is closed is technically absent though actually on the premises and so under a duty of care. Parents may be prosecuted if pupils are habitually late but the closing time of the registers needs to be made clear to staff and arrangements made for the late arrival of pupils to be recorded in some way so that their presence is known.

The onus on parents to see that their children attend is a strict one. In *Crump v Gilmore 1969* it was held that aunauthorised absence for even one session may create an offence and that it was no defence for parents to claim that they had done their best to see that the child attended, though in such circumstances help needs to be offered.

There are some defences available to parents if accused of breaking the law over attendance. The first is that the absence has indeed been authorised for one of the reasons given in the code above. The second is that on grounds of a day of religious observance set by the faith to which the child belongs, whether the absence is authorised or not. A third is the child's own sickness. A fourth is that free transport to school is an entitlement and it has not been provided. Finally, the reason may be for an 'unavoidable cause'. This is open to interpretation but case law holds that the cause must be in relation to the child and not to others so, for example, keeping a child away to look after others is not permitted – the law is there to see that children receive the education to which they are entitled.

In Scotland a pupil over 14 may be exempted from attendance at school because of home circumstances. School attendance is dealt with under S.30 and Ss. 35–42 of the Education (Scotland) Act of 1980.

Opting out

Under the Education Reform Act 1988 parents have the right to decide to apply for grant maintained status for their particular school. The process is popularly known as 'opting out'. Since this was introduced the number of schools attempting to opt out has grown steadily, though not all applications are successful. The general effect is to transfer final control of a school from the LEA to the DFE, thus giving governors more discretion in the running of their own affairs. The disadvantages include a school of this type being unable to use the services of the LEA in relation to curriculum support and legal advice. The transfer of almost absolute power to governors can have a disastrous effect on relationships, as was shown recently in events at one London school. The motives for applying for grant maintained status range from a genuine desire for self-goverment through the hope of financial benefits to a desire to avoid closure.

The initiative for opting out may come either from governors or parents but the final decision over application rests with the latter. Governors may pass a resolution to apply and this must be confirmed at a second meeting held not less that 28 days and not more than 42 days later. If parents start the process then a written request must be made to the governors and this must be supported by a number of parents at least equal to 20% of the number of pupils on roll if governors are to be required to hold a ballot.

Parents of pupils registered at the school are eligible to vote and an electoral roll must be prepared listing them, though name and address may be omitted at an individual's request. A copy of the roll must be available for any parent requesting it.

The Electoral Reform Society conducts the ballot. If at least 50% of parents vote and there is a simple majority in favour then the governors must go ahead with the application. Otherwise, a second ballot must be held within 14 days and this is decisive whatever the turn-out. If there is a majority in favour then the application goes forward for approval or rejection by the Secretary of State.

Regulations for applying for grant maintained status are contained in Ss.60–63 of the 1988 Act and the DFE publishes a booklet: *School Governors: How to become a Grant Maintained School* (1991).

Further reading

As well as the additional material mentioned throughout this chapter the Advisory Centre for Education publishes a number of booklets relating to parental rights. The law relating to special needs is dealt with comprehensively in *The Law of Special Educational Needs* by Bryan Cox (1986) and published by Croom Helm.

12 Safety, premises and transport

The extension of self-government and management to schools has brought with it increased responsibility for school premises. In law, by the way, 'premises' does not just mean buildings, it includes all that is within the boundaries of a property so that play areas and sports fields have to be considered.

Already, we have discussed the legal responsibilities to be undertaken when pupils are in the care of schools and teachers but there are wider implications affecting all who visit a school, whether pupils, staff, parents or visitors. The two main areas of law which concern their safety are under **Health and Safety** and **Occupier's Liability**.

Health and safety

The Health and Safety at Work Act was passed in 1974 and is a part of criminal legislation. Before this time, apart from an occupier's liability, the only major legislation relevant to safety in schools was the Offices, Shops and Railways Act of 1963 which related to certain ancillary staff working in school offices. Apart from some limited directives from the DFE or LEAs, no standards were required to ensure the health and safety of others lawfully on school premises, whether staff or pupils. Of course, there was always the right for injured parties to sue for compensation under the tort of negligence but, as we have seen, it is difficult and expensive to bring such an action. Health and safety legislation has changed all this.

The Act requires employers to take all reasonable steps for the health and safety of all who work at a school and all who have a legitimate right to be there. It is not, therefore, a counsel of perfection but a means of creating an awareness of safety factors and putting pressure on those who fail to make positive efforts to respond.

Under the Act the Secretary of State for Employment has power to create minor legislation in the form of Regulations and these are binding upon schools. These are supplemented by numerous Codes of Practice which, although not legally binding, one ignores at one's peril.

Administration is by the Health and Safety Executive on behalf of the Health and Safety Commission and enforced through an inspectorate and, if necessary, by prosecution. The main features may be summarised thus:

1 The legislation covers all aspects of health and safety.

2 It applies to all lawfully on premises where work takes place.

3 It is part of the criminal law.

4 Codes of Practice are issued which employers are expected to follow.

5 There are inspectors who have wide powers of enforcement.

6 Records must be kept and serious accidents and outbreaks of disease reported.

7 There is a right for safety representatives to be appointed in each workplace.

Regulations

These are in the form of Statutory Instruments and are mandatory. A good example is found in the requirement for reports where there has been an injury, outbreak of disease or what is termed a 'dangerous occurrence'. Consider these incidents which all took place in schools:

A teacher, Mr A, slipped on a polished floor and broke his leg. He would be off school for some time. A boy (Charles), attempting to close an upstairs classroom window, leaned out and fell some distance to the ground below. Surprisingly, he was unhurt. A boy (David) ran along a school corridor and straight through a glass window, severed an artery and died. A girl (Elizabeth) using pointed scissors in a needlework lesson stabbed herself in the eye. A teacher (Miss B) had contracted tuberculosis.

All these incidents required the completion of reports to be submitted to both the employer and the Health and Safety Executive. This is under The Reporting of Injuries, Diseases and Dangerous Occurrences Regulations 1985. These require the reporting of any accident leading to an employee being off work for longer than three days (Mr A); a dangerous occurrence, even where no injury results (Charles); a fatality (David); and any disease likely to affect others at the place of work (Miss B).

Some of these needed to be reported under more than one heading. The report should be followed by contact from the employer and from the inspectors of Health and Safety, not with a view to apportioning blame but of giving advice as to how accidents might be avoided in the future. The reports will certainly put pressure on employers to take action where that is needed. The head is responsible for submitting such reports and this is normally on forms provided for the purpose.

Codes of Practice

These give details of good practice to be followed in a number of areas affecting the health and safety of those in places of work and it is the responsibility of employers to see that the Codes are made known to those in management positions and to other employees. Although they are not mandatory the Codes have a strong influence and breach of them is clear evidence that the employer has failed to act reasonably. Schools need to follow them wherever possible. There are many but those likely to be of relevance to schools concern laboratories, use and storage of dangerous chemicals, use of electrical equipment, fire hazards and the handling of machines in workshops. If necessary, the Codes and advice concerning them may be obtained from the Health and Safety Executive itself.

Checks and inspections

The onus is on the employer to see that checks are carried out but this duty may be delegated to those responsible for the management of particular sites, though the employer will not be able to avoid final responsibility if things go wrong. Heads will then be responsible for seeing that checks are carried out.

The detailed checking will have to be carried out by other staff so some form of internal reporting will be necessary to provide evidence that such action has been taken and to reveal hazards and areas of concern. Most LEAs issue forms for the purpose. One, say, will concern science laboratories with a list of items to be checked such as chemical storage, fume cupboard and gas and electrical equipment. Checking will be carried out by the head of science and colleagues and the result will go to the head who will take any possible internal action. The information will then go to the LEA's safety officer, indicating areas where the LEA should take action. The head, or a designated member of staff, needs to keep copies of checks carried out, together with dates and a record of action taken.

The checking of main curriculum areas in secondary schools and of classrooms in all schools is relatively easy to deal with. Heads need to remember, however, that checking needs to include corridors, cloakrooms, toilets and all general areas. Fire-fighting equipment and electric plugs need particular attention. Electrical equipment used by various members of staff in different areas should be another cause for concern.

All places covered by the legislation are open to inspection by inspectors of the Health and Safety Executive. They have right of access to any part of the premises. They may inspect machinery, equipment and documents. They may take photographs. They have power by use of prohibition notices to stop the use of particular equipment – perhaps a guillotine which does not have a guard. By the use of improvement notices they may require action to be taken within a specified time – perhaps the resiting of fire-fighting equipment. Finally, they may bring prosecutions.

Prosecutions

Since the Health and Safety Act is a criminal one a breach of it may result in prosecution in a magistrates court, though the aim of the legislation is not to seek out criminals and bring them to court but rather to put pressure on employers to make places of work as safe as possible. Either the employer or the worker may be prosecuted but heads and other teachers have little to fear if they use reasonable care, since the ultimate responsibility lies with the employer. Prosecutions relating to schools seem to run at about half a dozen a year but, to the best of the writer's knowledge, there has only been one prosecution of a teacher since 1974. Prosecutions might occur in the following circumstances:

Employer – is made aware of the hazard, receives a warning and takes no action.

Head – receives a clear direction from the employer and makes no effort to carry it out or is grossly negligent in doing so.

Teacher – receives a clear instruction from the head and either wilfully ignores it or is grossly negligent in carrying it out.

The employer could take disciplinary action against the head or teacher in either case.

Safety representatives

The members of each recognised union in a school are entitled to appoint a safety representative and the employer is required to cooperate with that person in making arrangements over health and safety matters. The legal basis is to be found in the Safety Representative and Safety Committee Regulations of 1977 and there is a Code of Practice and guidance notes available. Since a number of unions may have members in any one school there could, in theory, be a quantity of representatives. In practice, unions will usually agree on the nomination of one person and the regulations do not preclude any employee being nominated, even one who is not a union member at all.

Safety representatives have a right to:

- make inspections;
- investigate potential hazards and dangerous incidents;
- investigate complaints by employees;
- make representations to employers over health and safety matters;
- take part in any meetings concerning health and safety on the site;
- receive information from inspectors and be consulted by them;
- have time off work for recognised training.

If all this sounds rather forbidding, it needs to be noted that safety representatives cannot be held liable in law for accidents that may occur or for failing to perform their duties, or for performing them badly.

First aid and medical treatment

Employers are required to see that there is appropriate provision in a school of first aid material. This should be available at some central place and also at points of particular danger such as workshops, gymnasia, kitchens and laboratories. The materials should be contained in clearly labelled boxes and the contents should be basic since the provision of more sophisticated equipment might encourage unsuitable action to be taken by untrained persons.

Schools do not have to have a trained, qualified first aider present, indeed it would be impossible for many to meet such a requirement. However, even the smallest school should have someone appointed to take action when first aid is needed and to ensure the provision and availability of materials.

Basically, the position of teachers is that of responsible parents who would give first aid but, if there was a possibility of complications, would seek help from a doctor or call an ambulance. However, the presence of a trained first aider on a staff is highly desirable and many LEAs provide training courses or allow time off for staff to take courses with organisations such as the Red Cross.

There is always the temptation for those giving first aid to go too far and this should be strongly resisted. Negligence may lie not only in failing to take action but in taking the wrong action.

Each school needs to have one or more persons responsible for giving first aid and this needs to be made known to pupils and staff. In addition there needs to be someone who will make a decision as to whether further treatment is necessary, an ambulance called and parents informed. This person should also be responsible for maintaining records of accidents that occur and action taken. In small schools that person will almost certainly be the head, in a large school it could easily be an ancillary with first aid or even nursing qualifications.

A problem for schools is often the need to take swift action in the interests of the child and also to make parents aware of what is happening. If the treatment is basic then a note to parents informing them of this and suggesting a visit to their doctor if there are further worries should be sufficient. If hospital examination or treatment is necessary then every effort needs to be made to contact parents but this should not delay obtaining specialist help. Inevitably, some parents will be dissatisfied with the action taken or not taken so it is wise to be somewhat over- cautious. If a school has behaved in the circumstances as a responsible parent would do then no blame can be attached.

A particular problem may arise when parties are away on school visits. When parental consent for a visit is obtained it can easily include consent for staff to authorise medical treatment in emergencies. For older pupils the position has been eased by the judgment in the Gillick case.

Readers will remember that this turned on the giving of advice on contraception to those under the age of consent. The court, in dismissing Mrs Gillick's action, declared that there is no definite age up to which parental rights supersede those of a minor. The interests of a child must come first and where that child is genuinely capable of understanding the nature of a problem he or she may make a decision accordingly. The inference is that older pupils may make decisions over straightforward medical treatment.

Fire alarms and bomb scares

It does seem strange that if a school hall is used for public entertainment then it must be licensed and comply with strict regulations over fire hazards and must have a fire certificate after inspection by local fire officers yet there are no regulations concerning its use by, say, 600 pupils at a morning assembly.

Regulations over fire in places of work have not yet been applied to schools though the Education (School Premises) Regulations of 1981 do lay down requirements over the design of schools in relation to danger from fire. This does not mean that schools do not have to take great care over prevention of fire and action to be taken if an outbreak occurs but it may mean that some become complacent. Here is a checklist that could be applied to any school:

1. Have the arrangements been reviewed recently? Circumstances change and a review is necessary at least annually.
2. Has all fire-fighting equipment been checked recently and is a regular system of checks in operation? Is the siting of equipment appropriate with regard to likely hazards?
3. Are staff aware of how to use this equipment if necessary?
4. Is the alarm system working? It needs to be checked regularly.
5. Are escape routes and alternatives identified clearly for each area of the building? Are notices displayed in those areas?
6. Are all staff and pupils aware of the action to be taken if fire breaks out? Who calls the fire brigade?
7. Are assembly points clearly identified and are there clear arrangements for checking the presence of pupils and staff?
8. Are fire drills held regularly, both with and without warning?
9. Are fire regulations complied with over public performances? These usually apply to exits, seating and stage lighting.
10. Have local fire officers been asked to review the arrangements and give advice?

Bomb scares are usually hoaxes but they can cause great anxiety for a head who has to decide, say, whether to bring out a school on the opening day of GCSE examinations. Most LEAs expect the head to contact the police, ask for advice and then make a decision. There may be good reasons why the call is considered to be hoax – the voice may obviously be that of a pupil – but any serious doubt must lead to evacuation and this is best carried out by using the fire drill procedure.

If the head decides to evacuate and have the premises searched then both police and fire brigade must be informed and only volunteer staff should be involved, certainly not pupils.

Under the Criminal Law Act of 1977 the making of a hoax bomb call is an offence and if the culprit can be traced then action should certainly be taken as a warning to others.

Employers, head and teachers

We can now summarise the main responsibilities of these three with regard to health and safety matters:

Employer

Set out a general statement of safety policy
(*Safety Policies in the Education Sector* HMSO gives advice)
Appoint safety committees
Agree to appointment of safety representatives
Pass on information
Give advice and training

Head

Follow employer's instructions
Provide information for staff and pupils
Cooperate with safety representatives
Maintain procedures for first aid and medical emergencies
Lay down systems of checks and fire drills
Report and record accidents and hazards

Teacher

Act responsibly as an employee
Act responsibly as a good parent would
Follow the instructions of employer and head
Report potential hazards to head and safety representative
Be careful over use of dangerous equipment
Be aware of action to be taken in emergencies

Occupier's liability

Although there are two Acts of Parliament, those of 1957 and 1984, dealing with an occupier's liability to those on the premises in reality they are only aspects of the tort of negligence put in statutory form.

The 1957 Act lays down a common duty of care, as it is known, to all who have permission to be on premises or who are lawful visitors. All reasonable steps must be taken for their safety while carrying out the activities for which they have entered. Thus there is a common duty of care towards parents visiting a school on an open evening and a school would be in breach if one slipped on a dangerous floor and was injured. If, however, a parent decided to experiment with a piece of PE apparatus, this being unknown to staff, he would be exceeding the permission to visit the premises and there would be no liability if he was injured.

The Act recognises that greater care is necessary towards young children and also that specialist visitors, for example builders or electricians, may be expected to appreciate and guard against any risks peculiar to themselves. The Act does not apply to trespassers though measures should not be taken deliberately to hurt them. It does not require any special care to be taken over trespassing by children.

In the 1970s there were a number of cases involving child trespassers who were badly injured on building sites and railway lines and the judgments suggested that some duty of care should be owed to more vulnerable members of society, particularly by large firms and organisations, such as British Rail, which have the expertise and finance to cater for safety.

The Act of 1984 attempts to clarify this situation. It creates a duty of care towards trespassers where the occupier is aware that trespassing takes place or can reasonably be expected to know that this might be so. If that is the case then the occupier must take reasonable steps to guard against dangers to possible trespassers. The difficulties lie in deciding whether the occupier could be expected to know of the trespassing and whether a particular danger ought to have been foreseen. There might well be liability for a school in the following case:

An infants' school has an 'adventure playground'. One piece of equipment is broken and potentially dangerous so pupils are not allowed to use it and supervisors ensure that they do not do so. Repairs have not been carried out by the weekend. The head is well aware that very small children from an adjoining estate trespass by getting through a hole in the boundary fence which has been there for some time. On Saturday afternoon a small child comes onto the playground and is injured by the defective equipment.

The possibility of trespass by easy access was known and the likely harm could have been foreseen. Even if there was no record of previous trespassing there might be liability since the hole in the fence was allowing a distinct possibility of this happening. It could be argued, of course, that the negligence was that of the parents in not exercising proper supervision of the child.

For trespassing adults and older pupils warning notices may provide a useful defence but they carry very little weight where very young children are involved.

Who is the occupier? The answer in law is not always clear since in some circumstances even squatters may be occupiers. Normally, employees cannot be occupiers since the assumption is that they occupy through the employer so the liability in schools seems to lie with the LEA or, in the case of aided, special agreement and grant maintained schools, with the governors. Certainly, the head is not the occupier but has a clear duty to report all potential risks to the employer.

Trespass on premises

All schools have problems over trespass. As we pointed out earlier, trespass is a tort – a civil wrong – so trespassers may not be prosecuted under the criminal law unless they commit some other act such as criminal damage. A sign that says **Trespassers will be prosecuted** is nothing more than a deterrent. Remedies for trespass are an action for damages or an injunction preventing further repetition. Until 1982 that was the position for schools.

The Local Government (Miscellaneous Provisions) Act 1982 S.40 has changed the position for schools. This creates a new criminal offence. This is committed where a person enters educational premises as a trespasser, or remains after having been declared a trespasser, and causes a nuisance or disturbance. The law applies both day and night and to all parts of a school or college property.

The offence is not an arrestable one but police may certainly be called to deal with it and use reasonable force to eject the trespasser. Prosecutions may be brought by the LEA of maintained schools or the governors of other schools or, by agreement, by the police. Parents have an implied right to visit schools but once declared to be trespassers they must leave or the offence is committed. To the writer's knowledge successful prosecutions have been brought against parents, excluded pupils, suspended teachers and others.

Licensing

If schools are to be used outside normal hours then licensing is only required if the public are admitted or alcohol is to be sold. What constitute the 'public' is not always clear in law but it can be said that if tickets for an event are sold in such a way that those unconnected with the particular school may have access then the public has been admitted. If entry is restricted to parents, pupils' relatives and staff then no licence is required. Regulations over Health and Safety still apply and so does the liability of the occupier.

Modern legislation encourages the use of school premises outside school hours both by schools and by the local community and the Education (No 2) Act 1986 S.42 gives control of such use to the governors of maintained schools, the governors of other schools already having such power. With the development of LMS and local financial control the income to be derived from letting the premises is attractive as well as its value in developing closer links with the community. Such use may well require licensing.

Public entertainment

The Local Government (Miscellaneous Provisions) Act 1982, mentioned earlier in relation to trespass, deals with this matter under S.1. It requires a licence to be obtained for public dancing, music or any similar form of entertainment or any indoor sporting events. The requirement applies even if no entry fee is charged. There is no clear definition of events that are included but certainly dances and concerts have to be licensed but fairs, jumble sales, quizzes and debates do not. The local district council may apply the law to outside events of a musical nature if it wishes.

Although the Government has stated that the legislation was not intended to apply to schools, as matters stand it does so and schools should not advertise an event widely or admit the general public unless a licence has been obtained.

Applications should be made to the local district council and at least 28 days notice given and both police and fire authority informed. The application may be for an annual or occasional licence and the fee is a matter for the council. Appeal against refusal may be made to the Magistrates Court. Both police and fire officers have right of entry to the premises to see that the terms of the licence are being complied with.

Schools concerned over licensing and public entertainment should check with the LEA and the local district council and consult the Home Office publication *Public Entertainment Licensing and School Premises*. The head must see that the conditions of the licence are met where the school organises the event and, if the organisation is from outside, that those responsible are aware of those conditions.

Dramatic performances

When plays or other dramatic performances take place in schools and the public may attend then the law is similar to that for public entertainments except that the legislation is to be found in the Theatres Act 1968. The local district council issues the licence and police and fire officers have right of entry to see that its terms are complied with. Fire officers pay particular attention to stage performances and hazards over seating, escape routes, curtains and stage and auxiliary lighting. Usually, they will visit a school well beforehand to check the arrangements.

Alcohol

Since the passing of the Licensing (Occasional Permissions) Act 1983 it has been possible for organisations which do not operate for private gain, such as PTAs, to apply for up to four occasional licences per year for the sale of alcohol at their functions. The application must be made at least a month beforehand to the licensing justices of the area in which the event is to be held.

Whenever there is a question of licensing it is always important to contact the local district council since detailed arrangements vary and they have power to decide – some make no charges for schools at all.

Lotteries

Small lotteries and raffles may take place during any event such as a fair, dance or jumble sale without any fuss though the draw must be held at the time, cash prizes are not allowed and after expenses proceeds must not be for private gain. No permission is necessary.

A private lottery, i.e. one restricted to members of an organisation such as a PTA may also be held without permission though the promoter must have authority in writing from, say, the PTA committee and there must be no private gain involved. Tickets must bear the name and address of the promoter, details of persons to whom tickets may be sold and a statement to the effect that prizes will only be given to the actual holders of winning tickets. Tickets must not be sent through the post.

Larger lotteries involving sale of tickets to those outside an organisation or beyond those attending a function are subject to legal control under the Lotteries (Amendment) Regulations 1981. These require registration with the local authority and payment of a fee. The regulations are quite complicated and advice should be taken from the local council before becoming involved, particularly when pupils are involved, since the sale of tickets to those under 16 is forbidden. Tickets may not be sold in the street.

Minibuses

Many schools today have their own transport, usually in the form of a minibus, and this raises problems of both safety and licensing.

If a minibus, which is defined as a vehicle seating eight to 16 passengers, is operated without charges being made to those who ride in it, then the law relating to it is the same as for private cars with regard to insurance and licensing. Owners and drivers are open to prosecution or suits in negligence in the normal ways.

If charges are made for passengers then the position changes. Under the Transport Act 1985 S.19 educational, religious and social welfare organisations may apply for a permit to operate and charge without being bound by regulations applying to public service vehicles. They are, however, bound by other regulations.

Permits are under the control of the Traffic Commissioners who may issue permits or allow LEAs or other responsible bodies to do so. Those bodies may issue their own regulations and LEAs usually do so. The permit itself must name the organisation, the number of the vehicle and the class of passengers to be carried. A disc is issued with the permit and this must be displayed on the windscreen. Since permits relate to individual vehicles then each must carry a disc.

Since owners are responsible for the safety and maintenance they may make any additional rules that they wish. Those under 21 may not drive in any case but a restriction of at least five years' driving experience could be made or a requirement of practice with the vehicle before carrying pupils could be insisted upon. Staff asking to drive should always be asked to complete a statement regarding their driving experience and any record of accidents or prosecutions. In cases of doubt, permission should be refused. It should be made clear who might be carried in the vehicle and it must not, in any case, be used to transport pupils to and from school on a regular basis.

There are complicated regulations over such matters as seating, exits, first aid, fuel tanks, lighting and so on. Manufacturers now produce vehicles which comply with these regulations so the safest course is to buy one of these. Schools contemplating conversions of vehicles should check the regulations carefully with the Traffic Commissioners. Most teacher unions can give detailed advice over this and the use of minibuses generally.

Further reading

Selwyn's *Health and Safety at Work*, published by Butterworths, gives full general information. *Health and Safety in Schools* by Barry Stock (1991), published by Croner, relates the legislation to schools. There are a number of DFE publications – one relating to safety generally in schools and others relating to safety in outdoor education, laboratories, practical studies, workshops and PE.

Test yourself

1 Health and Safety legislation is criminal and therefore the purpose is to seek out erring employers and punish them. True or false?

2 In Health and Safety law what is the difference between a Regulation and a Code of Practice?

3 Because of defective equipment a child is injured in a classroom and a breach of health and safety is alleged. The employer blames the head. The head blames the teacher. The teacher blames the other two and the safety representative. Where does the responsibility lie?

4 The staff car park is at the rear of a large school. It may only be reached by a road alongside a main block from which there are two exits for pupils. A pupil rushes out of one of these exits and is struck by a staff car. Fortunately, the car is moving very slowly but the pupil is bruised and cut and has to receive hospital treatment. What other action should the head take?

5 As a result of the incident above a Health and Safety inspector pays a visit. What action might he or she take?

6 Perhaps maliciously, the unions in a school agree to appoint Mr Redman as safety representative. He is not a member of any union and is believed by the head to be a trouble-maker. The head refuses to recognise the appointment and will not cooperate with Mr Redman. What is the position?

7 It is a bad day. A window cleaner slips and breaks an arm. At a parents' evening a male parent who has put on his best suit for the occasion rips this badly on a nail projecting from a seat in a lecture theatre. Another parent, unseen by staff, fiddles with a machine in a workshop and sustains a severe cut. What liabilities might have been created?

8 A primary school has problems of trespass by local teenagers. A warning sign says **No trespassing** and the gates are locked once school is over. Two 13-year-olds climb over the gates and, finding a window ajar, climb into a canteen. In attempting to heat baked beans one is burned by the gas stove which is in a faulty condition. Is the school liable in any way?

9 Mr X is a difficult parent who visits regularly to complain over numerous minor matters. One morning he arrives and alleges that his daughter is being bullied by other girls. The head listens patiently and says that this will be investigated. Mr X demands to speak to the girls involved and the head refuses. Mr X does not become aggressive or abusive but says that he intends to stay put until his request is granted and settles into a chair in the head's office. What action is open to the head?

10 The PTA decides, with the agreement of the head, to organise a dance in aid of school funds. Tickets are to be sold to members of the public and there is to be a bar. A raffle is to be held during the evening. What are the responsibilities of the head?

Comments will be found at the end of the book (page 209).

13 Finance and insurance

A school has always been required to deal with its finances in an orderly and accountable way but since its official funding was usually limited to a capitation allowance and a limited one for furniture, apparatus and equipment there was little room for virement and control was straightforward. Problems, if they did occur, were often with the handling of unofficial funds which were not directly under the control of the LEA.

Under the Education Reform Act 1988 schools have wide powers over finance allocated to them by the LEA or, in the case of grant maintained schools, by the DFE. This finance is determined in the following way:

General schools budget

This is the overall budget decided by the LEA. It has to cover all costs of administering the service for which it is responsible. There is some discretion as to which elements will be funded direct by the LEA and which will be funded by schools out of their allowances. Those which an LEA must retain itself include all capital expenditure and debt charges, specific government grants for training or initiatives such as TVEI, central administrative costs and school transport.

There are a number of items which the LEA may retain if it wishes or delegate to schools – finance being allocated accordingly. These will vary from one area to another. They include maintenance costs and those of repairs to buildings and equipment, insurance, child guidance and education welfare services, provision for statemented pupils, advisory services, supply cover and staffing costs relating to premature retirement and dismissal. School meals are included – some LEAs have already abandoned them completely – but this service has to be put out to private tender. Because of limits set by the Act it would be impossible for an LEA to retain all these to itself – it has to make choices.

Aggregated schools budget

This is the finance available after the LEA has decided on the discretionary items that it will keep to itself. A formula must be devised for allocating sums under the other headings to the schools and that formula must be based on pupil numbers, weighted by age, for at least 75% of its total. It must also allow for extra costs incurred for pupils with special learning difficulties and for the additional problems of small schools. Its provisions must be expressed simply and clearly to the schools themselves.

Delegated budget

This is the amount actually delegated to a school and over which it has control. The budgeting is a matter for the governors who are responsible for approving it and accounting for it though the administration of it will normally be under the control of the head. Here is an example of items delegated to schools by one LEA:

- Teaching and non-teaching salaries
- Supply cover
- Midday supervisors
- Foreign language assistants
- Support for statemented pupils (part)
- Non-structural maintenance of school buildings
- Grounds maintenance
- Energy costs
- Rent/rates/water charges/refuse collection
- Furniture and equipment
- School allowance (capitation) and exam fees
- Caretaking
- Cleaning

Contracts and tendering

The Local Government Act 1988 requires local authorities to put out for competitive tendering contracts for school catering, cleaning and general maintenance. The local labour force may put in tenders for these in competition with any others who wish to apply.

The basic situation is that, apart from the items mentioned, schools are free to make contracts without competitive tendering over areas where finance has been delegated to them, though in the interests of economy it may well be wise to do so. Since these items will vary from one area to another, it is necessary to consult the LMS scheme which, by law, each LEA must produce. Competitive tendering would certainly not be advisable over emergency repairs.

Conditions

All this gives considerable freedom to schools to make decisions over their spending but there are conditions.

1. The governors and the head must observe the law as laid down in the 1986 and 1988 Acts. This takes priority over any statements in the LMS scheme or in the Instrument or Articles of Government.
2. Where the LEA or DFE is entitled to make regulations these must be followed, particularly over the need for good financial practice.
3. Where governors award payments over dismissal or premature retirement which is against an LEA's policy the cost may be charged to a school's budget. If governors act unreasonably over dismissal of staff then that may also be charged to the budget.
4. If governors fail to carry out work necessary for general maintenance or health and safety the LEA may step in, carry out work and charge the cost to the budget.
5. If governors fail to comply with the provisions of an LMS scheme or there is clear evidence of mismanagement then, under S.37 of the 1988 Act, delegated powers to a school may be withdrawn. There is a right of appeal to the Secretary of State against such an action.

Charging

The regulations relating to charging laid down in the 1988 Act have caused considerable problems for schools, particularly over educational visits. The basic principle is that education must be free if it takes place within school sessions or, if outside those sessions, it is required to meet the demands of the National Curriculum. An exception is individual tuition on a musical instrument, unless this is required under the National Curriculum. Since parents must be told of the timing of the school day they are able to work out for themselves whether an activity must be free or not.

Examples of instances where charges may not be made include visits during school hours, provision of materials for practical lessons and books. There is nothing to prevent parents from making voluntary contributions, of course, but this must be made clear to them. If more than 50% of an educational activity takes place outside school hours then a charge may be made if the visit it non-residential – a trip to a theatre which leaves school early would qualify. For residential visits the regulations are more complicated and may be found in S.109 of the 1988 Act.

Both LEA and governors must see that there is a policy over charging and that this is made known to parents. The accompanying table (Figure 9) shows one set up by one LEA. The DFE Circular: *Education Reform Act 1988: Charges for School Activities* gives advice.

Private funds

Since the LEA has provided public funding for schools then it must see that the handling of and accounting for those funds is efficient and without taint. Because of its general responsibility for schools it may also issue directions over the auditing of other school funds but it has no power to control the spending of those funds or dictate accounting procedures. These lie with the governors and head and it is here that inefficiency and even malpractice may occur, causing great embarrassment in a local community. A recent case concerned the head of a large school who had stolen large sums of money paid in by pupils for a foreign visit.

New Broom

A head took up post in a large school which was badly run in many ways. He examined the handling of finance and discovered that while funds from the LEA were handled meticulously by a competent office staff teachers were left to their own devices when it came to money for trips, concerts and charity events. Staff were collecting money from pupils to buy extra books and

Charging and Remissions Policy

	Issues	Policy
A	Residential Courses in school time – Board and Lodgings costs	Parents will be required to meet full cost except children whose parents receive income support/family credit, where charges should be remitted by school.
B	Activities outside school hours not within National Curriculum	Parents meet full cost.
C	Individual Music Tuition	No charge for the Authority's service but school may bring outside tutors in within school hours at a charge to parents. However, if part of National Curriculum, prescribed examination charges must be remitted.
D	Dual Examination Entries	Charge to parents.
E	Extra examinations entries/resits without tuition	Charge to parents.
F	Exams not on the prescribed list	Charge to parents.
G	'Wasted' exam entries	Parents charged when exam wasted without reason acceptable to school otherwise school pays.
H	Ingredients/materials for practical subjects	Parents will be encouraged to provide materials for practical subjects; but no child must be disadvantaged because of parents' inability/reluctance to pay. Where necessary, school will pay.
I	Lost school equipment, books etc.	Parents will be expected to replace or purchase lost items of school property.
J	Breakages and damage to school buildings, furniture or property	Parents to be made aware that wilful damage to school buildings or property will be charged to parents by the school.

Figure 9 Example of LEA charging policy – Derbyshuire LEA

using personal cheques to pay for them. Money was being kept in cocoa tins and there were at least half a dozen different accounts at a local bank and the Post Office, either in the names of individual members of staff or in the name of specific events. The previous head had been in the habit of handling cash himself. No receipts were given for money collected and no balance sheets were produced. Pupils paid money on a termly basis into a central school fund and this was spent at the discretion of the head. It was handled properly by office staff and audited by a governor with a commercial background but no balance sheet was produced publicly.

Accusations of dishonesty, if made, could not have been rebutted. The new head quickly sensed that many staff felt uneasy over the situation. He decided to take the following steps:

1 All accounts in the name of individuals or specific events were closed and several central funds established under the control of the office staff and the head himself.

2 Staff wishing to collect money for any purpose were required to obtain the head's permission and given procedures to be followed. The head himself would not handle money directly in any way at all but would carry out checks.

3 Pupils paying money to staff would have this clearly recorded. Where large amounts were involved parents would be advised to pay in person or by cheque and receipts would be given.

4 Staff would pay sums collected into a central fund and would be given a receipt by office staff. All payments to travel firms, bus companies, theatres and charitable organisations would be made from this fund.

5 A balance sheet would be required for each event and presented to the head. It would be filed and available to any parent who raised a query. Any surplus would be returned to parents or, if minimal, would be transferred to the general school fund.

6 The general funds would be audited by an independent volunteer or, if necessary, by a paid accountant. Staff and governors could not be involved since they had an interest (tact was needed in the explanation to the governor involved).

7 Pupils would be involved in decisions over the spending of termly donations to school funds.

8 A balance would be produced annually for the central funds and presented to governors, displayed on staff notice boards and copies made available for parents on request.

Tuckshops, vending machines and sale of other goods

Many schools will raise funds by other means. These three are common ones. All require proper control of finance, as with other private funds, and the production of balance sheets for governors and other interested parties. They raise other issues.

First, each will create contracts with the supplier of items to be sold, with all that that implies (as explained in Chapter 5). The head, who will often be one party to the contract, will need to have terms clarified. It needs to be remembered that contracts do not necessarily have to be in writing and that business arrangements always imply that a contract exists. Terms in writing are always advisable.

Second, legislation applying to the sale of food will apply. This covers the food itself and the premises from which it is sold. Schools are well advised to sell only packaged goods in tuckshops and vending machines since liability will then lie with the manufacturer unless the defect is readily recognisable.

Third, the Trades Descriptions Act, which is a criminal one, will apply. This may well be relevant if schools sell uniform and sports equipment. The goods must be in accord with any description given to parents or pupils.

Fourth, the Sale of Goods Act also applies. This is a civil one so prosecution is not possible but an action for damages could be brought. The goods sold must be of merchantable quality and reasonably fit for their purpose so schools need to check samples carefully before becoming involved.

PTAs and similar organisations

A school has no legal liability for such organisations. They exist as separate bodies and, at present, there is no obligation for governors to agree to their formation or use of the premises. The benefits they usually bring in terms of parental contact, goodwill and financial support can be so great that their activities need to be approved and encouraged. Often they will look to the head for advice.They need to join the National Confederation of Parent-Teacher Associations which will give advice on setting up a constitution and conducting their affairs. Those need to follow the lines adopted by a club or society with rules for the conduct of meetings, committees, power of the chair, handling of finance and so on. The head would be wise to maintain close contact for, while there may be no legal liability, misconduct by a PTA, particularly over finance, could be embarrassing locally for any school.

A PTA may decide to raise money for specific purposes or donate lump sums to a general school fund. The former is preferable. It gives objectives to be attained and parents will be able to see tangible rewards for their efforts. However, the purchasing should be done through school funds since most of the items bought will then be free of VAT. The head needs to see that equipment bought is suitable for school use on grounds of safety.

Trusts

Many schools which originate from religious foundations i.e. almost all voluntary or aided schools may have funds available because of the existence of a trust.

A trust is a legal arrangement whereby persons known as trustees hold property on behalf of and for the benefit of others. The property may be proceeds from the use of land, such as rents, or from investments. The trust is likely to be in the form of a trust deed which will spell out the terms of the trust but in some instances a deed may never have been drawn up or it may have been lost, in which case the creation of a trust may be implied by the Charity Commissioners from the information available. Church schools can check with the Commissioners or their local church authorities as to the position.

Only the trustees themselves have power to determine the use of funds created by the trust and that must be in accordance with the terms of the trust. Otherwise, governors and the head have no control over trust funds but once they are allocated they must be used for the purposes laid down by the trustees. They may have powers to allocate sums for specific purposes only.

Today, other schools are considering setting up trust funds based on contributions from parents as a means of raising additional finance. The Charity Commissioners will give details as to how this may be accomplished.

Insurance

As explained in the earlier chapter on contracts, insurance agreements form legally binding contracts of a particular type – the party insured must reveal all relevant details to the insurer or the contract will be invalid. Otherwise, insurances are ordinary contracts – payments are made in return for a promise to indemnify if certain events occur. As with other contracts, insurance agreements contain many clauses and conditions which need careful examination, particularly in relation to what is covered and what is excluded. While some agreements are better than others you tend to get what you pay for.

Schools need to have insurance to cover risks from fire, storm damage, flood, vandalism, burglary, theft and similar risks. Where the LEA takes responsibility it may well decide not to insure but to meet costs from contingency funds. If so, schools need take no action. Schools also need to have third party insurance, that is insurance against claims by others on grounds of negligence by staff or deficiencies in buildings or equipment. Staff themselves must be insured.

Schools may decide to take out personal accident insurance for pupils but that it not essential and may well be left to parents themselves. If a school is not negligent then there is no liability towards an injured pupil.

The cost of essential insurance is one of those items which LEAs may fund themselves or may delegate to schools to cover in their budgets. A common practice is for LEAs to finance insurance for major events but leave schools to cover minor incidents such as theft or vandalism, either directly or through the LEA's own insurance scheme. Some LEAs offer to include personal accident insurance for pupils but that is a matter for governors to decide. Governors and heads need to examine their own local schemes to see that all necessary cover is provided.

Further reading

Local Financial Management in Schools by P. Downes (1988), published by Blackwell. *Local Management of Schools* by B. Davies and C. Braund (1989), published by Northcote House.

14 The National Curriculum

Before 1988 the curriculum of state maintained schools was defined by law only in very vague terms. It had to be suitable according to a pupil's age, ability, aptitude and special educational needs. The actual material taught was left to schools themselves though a great deal of advice was forthcoming from the DFE, LEAs, educational institutions and pundits. The result was that while most schools devised a balanced curriculum for their pupils there were others where the interests of pupils were placed below those of political activists or theorists pursuing laudable goals by impractical and inappropriate means. The demerits of the few led to condemnation of the many. The result was a sudden outbreak of interest in education by politicians and the imposition of a National Curriculum.

General statements in earlier Acts of Parliament still apply but the legal basis for the National Curriculum is to be found in the Education Reform Act 1988 and the succession of minor enactments that followed and still continue to appear. All are explained in advisory material from the DFE.

Two bodies under the Act are charged with responsibility for advising schools. They are the National Curriculum Council (for Wales the National Curriculum Council for Wales) and the Schools Examination and Assessment Council. Their advice is subject to approval by the Secretary of State so in effect the DFE has central control of the National Curriculum. There is, however, no direct control of how the Curriculum is to be taught – that is still a professional matter for the head and teaching staff.

The requirement is for all maintained schools to provide a basic curriculum for all pupils of compulsory school age, plus religious education (not strictly part of the National Curriculum). This curriculum must:

- be broad and balanced;
- promote the spiritual, moral, cultural, mental and physical development of pupils at school and in society;
- prepare pupils for the opportunities, responsibilities and experiences of adult life.

There is no specified time for each subject, no specified teaching methods or materials and no requirement that timetables should be subject based. Schools may add other subjects as they wish.

Under the National Curriculum schools must prepare appropriate programmes of study. They must set attainment targets and assess standards of achievement. These must take place at certain key stages of a pupil's career, the years in which the majority of a group reach 7, 11, 14 or 16 years of age. The subjects are known as core subjects or foundation subjects and there is a statutory requirement for the provision of RE, though this existed long before 1988. The basic content of syllabuses in both core and foundation subjects is laid down but schools are free to amplify this. The material does not have to be taught under subject headings, it may be covered in cross-curricular arrangements.

We can summarise the requirements thus:

THE NATIONAL CURRICULUM

Core subjects	English, mathematics, science
Foundation subjects	History, geography, technology, art, music, PE, modern language (Sec. Schs.)
Religious education	Syllabus approved by the local Standing Advisory Council for Religious Education. Compulsory provision for collective worship
Attainment targets	Compulsory in core subjects. As appropriate in foundation subjects
Assessment	Tests at 7, 11, 14 and 16
Exceptions	May be made for individual pupils but parents have a right of appeal
External qualifications	Only those approved by the DFE to be taken

It is not possible here to deal with the detail of the National Curriculum which is subject to addition and change, as readers will be only too aware, but the following points need to be made:

1 Apart from the 1988 Act itself the detail of the National Curriculum is made compulsory by a succession of Statutory Instruments and these are followed by advisory Circulars which have a strong persuasive influence.

2 The provisions apply to all maintained schools. They do not apply to independent schools or to parents educating children 'otherwise' at home. City technology colleges must teach the core and foundation subjects as a condition of their grant.

3 The Secretary of State has powers to change the National Curriculum. Testing may be introduced (or abolished) in any foundation subject, the key stages varied or the actual content altered.

4 There is a legal duty on LEAs, governors and heads to see that the National Curriculum is implemented.

5 There are exceptions. Excusal in whole or in part may be made for special schools or for pupils with special educational needs, though parents have a right of appeal against such decisions and they must be subject to review.

6 Parents have a right to information regarding the performance in the tests of their own children. Schools must also publish the unadjusted results in aggregate of pupils at 11, 14 and 16.

7 Whether parents have a right to withdraw their children from elements of the National Curriculum, from testing for example, is not yet clear. It would seem unlikely.

Further reading

Apart from the statutory requirements and the advice in Circulars the DFE publishes: *National Curriculum – from Policy to Practice* (1989) which is a relatively simple guide. *Implementing The National Curriculum* by W. S. Fowler (1990), published by Kogan Page, summarises the main elements and relates them to management issues.

15 External relations

Schools operate under the law as laid down by Parliament and administered through the DFE, LEAs and governing bodies. We have discussed the implications of this in earlier chapters but, as every teacher knows, many of the most difficult problems facing schools originate from happenings outside. Schools have little control in such matters yet they are expected to deal with the consequences and observe the rights of the parties involved. In order to do so they need to understand something of the law in relation to the family, welfare and medical services, the police and the criminal courts and others.

Family law

This has always been a difficult area because of the tensions and emotions involved but the increase in divorce and single-parent families has made matters a great deal worse. The result has been a sweeping change in the law relating to children in the form of The Children Act 1989, the impact of which is just beginning to be felt.

The Act says little of parental rights; it emphasises parental responsibility. This does not cease even if parents separate, divorce or re-marry. The responsibility is to care for and raise a child to be a properly developed adult both physically and morally. The Act places the needs and welfare of the child first and lays down that wherever possible the wishes of the child must be taken into account together with the likely effect of decisions on his or her future well-being.

Such decisions will now be taken by the new Family Proceedings Courts. These operate at the level of Magistrates Courts and those sitting will be chosen from a special panel for the purpose. The courts are required to follow three basic principles:

1 Over any question regarding the upbringing of a child, that child's welfare must be the paramount consideration.

2 An order should only be made concerning a child if doing so is better for the child than making no order at all.

3 Since delay is likely to prejudice the welfare of a child the court must set timetables for the completion of proceedings.

In addition to observing these principles a court is required, when considering a decision relating to the upbringing of a child, to carry out what is known as a welfare checklist. This will be significant for schools.

Welfare checklist

1 What are the wishes and feelings of the child, bearing in mind age and understanding?
2 What are the child's physical, emotional and educational needs?
3 What is the likely effect of any change in the child's circumstances on him or her?
4 What is the relevance of the child's age, sex, background or other characteristics?
5 Has the child suffered any harm or is there a risk of this?
6 How capable are parents or others involved of meeting the child's needs?
7 Which powers of the court might be available and appropriate in this particular situation?

This list is not meant to be exhaustive.

Orders

The Act does away with the old concepts of custody and access and with Place of Safety Orders. These are replaced by the following orders:

Contact allows a person with whom the child does not live to have contact. The court decides whether this is face-to-face, by post or by telephone.

Prohibited steps bans any person with parental responsibility from taking any particular step without the consent of the court.

Residence settles arrangements over the person with whom a child is to live. One possible consequence is to give parental responsibility to step-parents. In effect this replaces the concept of custody.

Specific issue gives directions over a specific issue such as education or medical treatment.

There are two relating to child protection and these replace the old Place of Safety Orders:

Emergency protection enables a child's safety to be ensured. The order lasts for up to eight days and the local authority assumes parental responsibility.

Child assessment where Social Services consider a full assessment of a child's social and medical needs is necessary and parents refuse to cooperate. Parental responsibility is not given to the local authority.

Since schools often become embroiled in the tangle of relationships that may exist they need to make positive efforts to discover which orders relate to particular pupils and conditions laid down in those orders.

The Children Act and schools

Schools may be required under the Act to submit a report whenever a court is considering problems over a child's upbringing and here the welfare checklist given above will have to be used. Each child involved will be given a *guardian ad litem* – someone appointed to represent the interests of a child in court proceedings. This will usually be a social worker. This person has a right to the school report and to examine and copy any school records relating to the child. The report and records will be available to all parties concerned so they should not contain comments that cannot be substantiated. The timetable set by the court will have to be followed.

Since the Act replaces the concept of natural or adoptive parents with those having parental responsibility all those included have a right to be consulted as parents by schools. They include both natural parents (whether living together or not), divorced parents, step-parents and even those who have care of a child under, say, a residence order. All have a right to information regarding a child's work and progress unless that right has been removed by a court.

Sometimes schools are asked to change the name of a pupil. The Act forbids this unless all those with parental responsibility agree or a court authorises it. The agreement should be in writing. The exact name of the pupil and the date of birth may be uncertain. The correct details may be obtained from the birth certificate and schools may insist on seeing this. Birth certificates are public documents and, if there is refusal by parents or any doubt, copies may be obtained from the Registrar of Births, Deaths, and Marriages.

Schools may be faced with the problem of a parent who decides to remove a child from school, either in the short term or with the intention of educating the child at home. Previously, the position was that any parent with care and custody could take either of these steps. The Act does not seem clear over this matter but the writer suggests that only a person with a right to control a child's residence could take the step of short-term removal and that educating at home would require the consent of all with parental responsibility or permission of the court. Undoubtedly, there will be case law on this aspect and on others arising from implementation of the Act.

Attendance

The obligation on schools to reveal statistics on attendance and truancy means that vigilance over attendance is now even more important. It is still the responsibility of the education welfare service and parents may still be prosecuted and fined by magistrates. However, it is no longer possible for parents to be imprisoned for their failure to secure attendance.

A pupil whose attendance is unsatisfactory may be made the subject of an education supervision order by the Family Proceedings Court. This may not take place if a care order is in force and it lapses if a care order is made. If the supervision order is made then, on behalf of the court, the education welfare officer must monitor attendance and give help and advice to school and parents as necessary. Parents who fail to comply commit an offence and the result may be care proceedings.

We can now see how the new law might be applied to a particular situation in which a school had some involvement.

The Porter Family

Mr and Mrs Porter, after much bitter wrangling and some physical violence, are in process of being divorced. They have two children, Thomas aged 12 and Daisy aged 7. Both attend church schools because Mrs Porter has strong feelings about this. Mr Porter is not satisfied with the secondary school attended by Thomas because it entails considerable travelling and the boy appears unhappy and tired. Mr Porter would prefer Thomas to attend his local comprehensive along with his friends and he is prepared to challenge Mrs Porter over this. Generally, Daisy is doing well at school though sometimes she appears to be upset and confused. Thomas is not making good progress and is already establishing a reputation for being disruptive in class.

Mrs Porter has walked out on Mr Porter, taking the two children with her. Both are upset because they have an attachment to both parents. Mr Porter is angry and demands that the children return to him as he is still in the family home and intends to remain there if possible. Mrs Porter is staying with a friend in another town. Finally, until the divorce comes through, the parents agree that the children shall stay with grandparents so that they may continue to attend their schools but Mrs Porter lays down a condition that Mr Porter does not disturb the children by visiting them until matters are settled. She makes it clear also that she will fight to keep both of them permanently with herself once she has found accommodation locally.

Mrs Porter visits both schools, asking that Mr Porter is not allowed access to Thomas and Daisy and describing his conduct in vitriolic terms. Mr Porter also visits both schools, blackening his wife's character and demanding information regarding them.

Situations like this where home problems involve schools are common enough. How might the two children and their parents be treated under the new legislation since it seems that any amicable arrangement is unlikely?

Thomas

The Family Proceedings Court will require reports from the probation officer or social worker involved in the divorce proceedings and from the school. A *guardian ad litem*, independent of the parents, will be appointed to represent the boy's interests. The court will place the welfare of Thomas above that of his parents and, since he is 12, may well be able to make some assessment of his own wishes. The welfare checklist will be applied in an effort to decide what is best for him.

With which parent would he be happier, safer and more likely to grow into a balanced and responsible adult? How is he coping at his present school? Would a change to his local school, perhaps attended by friends and without the stress of travel, be beneficial for him? Such considerations would take precedence over Mrs Porter's wishes and Mr Porter's desire to keep Thomas with him.

The court does not have to make orders but that would seem necessary here as there seems little likelihood of agreement. It will have to decide on residence, which could be with either parent or even with grandparents – if that should happen they will also qualify for parental responsibility. It will also have to decide on contact for the parent, parents, or other close relatives who are not the subject of the decision on residence. It will need to decide the specific issue of the school to be attended by Thomas.

Daisy

Similar steps will have to be taken over the preparation of reports, the appointment of a *guardian ad litem* and the application of the welfare checklist. Even though Daisy is only 7, an effort must be made to discover her feelings and wishes and a great deal will depend on her maturity for her age. Would a separation from her mother be wise at such an early age? Would Mr Porter be able to cope satisfactorily with her upbringing?

Again, the court would have to decide on questions of residence and contact. The question of school is not yet a problem – it could have been if Mrs Porter's final move entailed a change of school – but the issue will crop up again when Daisy is old enough to transfer from primary school.

The schools

Whatever the court decides, both parents will have parental responsibility and if either re-marries that will extend to step-parents if Thomas or Daisy are resident with them. Even the grandparents would have gained parental responsibility if either Thomas or Daisy were resident with them. All these would be entitled to the rights conferred upon parents by legislation – to information regarding school and the work and progress of the children for example. It would be most important for the decisions of the court to be known by both schools so that a careful observance of parental rights could be maintained, without sides appearing to be taken over the issues between the parties.

If Mrs Porter has either Thomas or Daisy resident with her and she re-marries then she may wish a change of surname on school records and registers. Although a child may be referred to by another name at home or by friends or relatives the only name that may be used on school records and examination entries is that on the birth certificate. The Children Act is specific about this under S.13(1)(a), thus removing some doubts created by case law. The written agreement of all with parental responsibility must be obtained before such a change is made or the court has given permission. If the court is involved then that will amount to a specific issue and the welfare checklist will have to be applied.

Child protection

Children may be at risk in many ways. The reforms brought about by The Children Act go some distance in the protection of children in ways that have been described but there are existing elements in the law that remain in force, particularly in relation to physical and moral risks.

A number of cases in recent years relating to physical and sexual abuse of children have revealed the extent of the problems in our society though whether these have increased or have always been present to the same extent under the surface is open to question. The result has been increasing public concern and the need for schools to be more vigilant since they are often able to spot signs of abuse at a relatively early stage.

Local authorities, through their Social Services departments, are required to investigate and, if necessary, deal with suggestions of child abuse that are brought to their attention. Their investigations may lead to the use of any of the orders available under The Children Act as well as prosecutions under the criminal law. They are required to keep a register of children known to be at risk, or suspected of being so, and to monitor the behaviour and treatment of these children. There should be close liaison with schools and the schools themselves should know which pupils are on the at risk register, possibly with a member of staff responsible for contact with social workers involved.

However, schools need to be careful over assuming that some form of abuse has taken place since an allegation without real substance could lead to an action in defamation by those accused. Children do fantasise and tell stories to impress others. Bruises do not necessarily imply parental violence. Perhaps cruelty by neglect is easier to recognise. If the evidence is obvious, or there is a repetition of minor incidents, the correct procedure is to alert the local Social Services or the NSPCC Advice to schools in such matters is given in DFE Circular 4/88: *Working together for the protection of children from abuse: procedures within the education service.*

Any person may report suspected cruelty towards children of any kind to the NSPCC which then has an obligation to investigate – almost all the Society's enquiries stem from such reports – and schools should not hesitate to make contact, especially where the difficult element of sexual abuse may be concerned. This needs tactful handling by trained enquirers. The Society is prepared to give advice on signs of possible sexual abuse that may be evident from the behaviour of children at school, for example a fear of medical examination, a great reluctance to change for PE or a knowledge of sexual matters far beyond that which could be expected.

Schools need to consider carefully matters of confidentiality and access to records in relation to suggestions or suspicions of cruelty or abuse.

Child guidance

Under the 1981 Act LEAs have a responsibility to provide for the special educational needs of pupils and, for those with less severe special needs, a similar responsibility lies upon governors. How this is to be provided is very much a local matter and under schemes of local management or opting out schools may be required to pay for some of these services out of their delegated budgets. In the event of parental complaint that help is not being provided in accordance with the Act schools must be able to show that reasonable efforts have been made to obtain help from beyond their internal resources.

Those reasonable steps could be the involvement of specialist advisers and peripatetic teachers employed by most LEAs, or referral to an educational psychologist or a psychiatrist. Distinction between the last two is not always easy to define except that the former is employed by an LEA and the latter by the health service. Broadly speaking, the psychologist deals with learning problems rather than those of behaviour, though often the two will be inextricably linked. The psychiatrist deals mainly with emotional and behavioural problems.

An example of how a problem might be tackled could be taken from what is known as 'school phobia' – a refusal to attend school. This should be approached in the first place by contact with the parents and the assistance of the education welfare officer, not as a means of threatening parents but as a low-key effort to find an answer – perhaps Johnny is being bullied on the school bus but is afraid to admit it. It may be that Johnny cannot cope with the work at school, or fears that he can't, and so referral to the psychologist might help. There may be deep-seated emotional problems that only a trained psychiatrist is able to diagnose. There may be need to refer Johnny to a child guidance clinic and this step may be taken by either the psychologist or the psychiatrist. Otherwise, their advice on treatment in school must be followed as far as possible.

Medical

The district health authority is responsible for health matters in schools and is expected to work closely with the LEA. It must appoint a school medical officer who is responsible locally for arranging medical inspections in schools, including those by nurses. Schools must provide adequate facilities for these inspections to be carried out. Through the school medical officer schools may insist on medical examinations for pupils, for example where there is a refusal to take part in PE, though parents have a right for these to be carried out by the family doctor if they wish.

When schools have problems over matters such as the period of exclusion for particular infections then the advice of the school medical officer should always be sought though the final decision will lie with the head.

Other services provided through the district health authority include the provision of routine dental inspections and free dental treatment, child guidance clinics, speech therapy, physiotherapy and assistance with school programmes on health education.

Juvenile crime and the police

There are two aspects of concern here for schools. The first concerns pupils who are in trouble over the commission of criminal offences and the second that of the powers of the police, particularly with regard to their powers to enter schools and question pupils.

Juvenile crime

A crime is an offence stated to be such by statute or under the common law. It may range from petty theft to murder. In essence, it is an offence against the community rather than against an individual and so, normally, prosecution is undertaken by the Crown Prosecution Service on behalf of the State, the case being dealt with in the criminal courts which may impose criminal sanctions. LEAs may prosecute parents for not sending children to school or for trespass on educational premises. Governors of aided schools may also bring prosecutions for trespass on their premises. With very few exceptions, the prosecution must prove that the criminal act was committed and that there was an intent to commit that act. The burden of proof lies upon the prosecution, who must prove guilt beyond any reasonable doubt.

The age of criminal responsibility in England and Wales is ten – in Scotland it is eight – so the majority of primary school children cannot be prosecuted. They are said to be incapable of forming the necessary criminal intent. When a child under ten does commit a serious offence, for example the killing of other small children, then recourse has to be had to care proceedings, which inevitably lead to secure confinement to prevent harm to others. Between the ages of ten and 14 children may be prosecuted but the onus is on the prosecutor to show not only that the act was committed but that the offender understood the nature of it and the fact that it was criminal. Prosecutions for crimes such as fraud and blackmail are thus most unlikely.

Between the ages of 14 and 17 there are no such restrictions though, with the exception of homicide, juveniles will be tried at special sittings of a magistrates' court for which there are particular rules. These include the use of magistrates from a special panel (at least one man and one woman must be included), no access to the general public and no reporting of names in the press unless authorised specifically by the court. Efforts are made to keep the hearings as informal as possible. If a juvenile under 17 is charged jointly with someone over that age then the case will be dealt with in the open magistrates' court but the juvenile, if found guilty, will be sent to a juvenile hearing for sentencing. Trials for homicide must take place in the Crown Court.

Before making a decision over sentence the magistrates will consider background material relating to juveniles before them and this will include reports from any schools concerned. The contents of such reports must be made known to the juvenile and those with parental responsibility so great care needs to be taken over their accuracy. Teachers may be called as witnesses. Juveniles may have legal representation or, at the discretion of the court, may be advised by parents or other responsible persons.

Sanctions available in juvenile courts are similar to those in other criminal courts though the terms 'conviction' and 'sentence' are replaced by 'finding of guilt' and 'order upon a finding of guilt'. An absolute discharge or a conditional discharge may be given. The former means that guilt is recorded but no punishment is given, the latter that guilt is not punished but some condition is laid down. Fines may be imposed and in many cases parents required to pay. Orders relating to supervision or community service may be imposed or the juvenile taken into care of the local authority or some other responsible person. Older juveniles may be given a term of youth custody but no person under the age of 21 may be sent to prison.

Schools should be informed of the result of cases concerning their pupils and this usually takes place through liaison between social workers and the education welfare officer, who will have been responsible for obtaining school reports.

Police

TV addicts might well have the impression that the main function of the police is to catch criminals. In fact, their main duties are to protect life and property and uphold the criminal law. In many areas there are good relationships between schools and the police who assist with aspects of the curriculum and give help and advice over security and other matters. In others there is distrust and animosity, particularly where LEAs have forbidden schools to allow police onto the premises, even in plain clothes. Schools need to establish good relationships with the police to help keep pupils out of trouble and encourage a respect for law and order within the local community. Play schemes organised by the police during school holiday periods have done much to help in this respect.

Strictly speaking, any known crime should be reported to the police. They would not be pleased with the head who reported a pupil for stealing sweets from another, even though that is theft. Where, however, a pupil commits a more serious offence such as an assault causing real harm then the police may well have to be involved. That option must certainly be given to the parents of the other child who has been attacked or a member of staff who has been hurt.

Cain and Abel

Two boys were scuffling in the playground of a secondary school. Each lost his temper and a real fight ensued. Before they could be separated by a teacher each had suffered bruises and minor cuts. They were given first aid. The senior teacher who dealt with the incident concluded that both were to blame and, with the head's approval, placed both on report to be of good behaviour. Letters were sent to Mr and Mrs Cain and Mr and Mrs Abel explaining what had happened.

Both sets of parents were upset and came to school to protest, each alleging that the other boy was to blame and had started the fight. Although still dissatisfied, Mr and Mrs Cain accepted the situation but Mr and Mrs Abel did not. They went to the police.

There can be no doubt that in this incident criminal offences may have been committed, in the form of assault and battery at the very least, though each party might have pleaded self-defence. The head could have informed the police but decided instead to approve an internal punishment and inform the parents, leaving it open to them to take further action if they wished. When Mr and Mrs Abel went to the police the police would have to investigate and report to the Crown Prosecution Service who would then decide whether to prosecute or not. It is just possible that as a result of the investigation both boys might have been prosecuted.

The incident is a real one (disguised of course) and in the event the decision was not to prosecute. Mr and Mrs Abel then decided to bring a private prosecution and Mr and Mrs Cain were so incensed that they took similar action. The court dismissed both and the parents were faced with the costs involved.

Under normal conditions police have no more right to be on school premises than, say, parents or other visitors. However, if an offence has been committed, or if police suspect that one is likely to take place, then they have a right of entry in order to investigate and to obstruct them is in itself an offence. If police ask to interview pupils then difficulties arise since the head is acting as parent and must behave accordingly.

The Police and Criminal Evidence Act 1984 led to new guidelines being issued to the police over the interviewing of juveniles. Unless a serious offence has been committed or is likely to take place and delay in questioning would have serious consequences, police are told to interview juveniles in the presence of their parents and preferably at home. If the police are in breach of these guidelines without good cause then a court may refuse to allow the evidence obtained to be presented.

If police insist on interviewing a pupil at school the head cannot refuse but should register a protest, insist on being present in place of the parent, log the incident and report it in writing to the LEA. If a girl pupil is being questioned then a policewoman should be present or a female member of staff if the head is a man. If the enquiry relates to possible child abuse or cruelty by parents then the police should be accompanied by a social worker and it would be wrong of the head to try to prevent interviewing since the child may be at risk. Here the safety of the child is more important than the rights of parents.

If police have a warrant to arrest a pupil then they have every right to make that arrest on school premises or anywhere else.

Employers

Schools will make many informal contacts with employers over careers and links related to the curriculum. There will also be the need to prepare references for pupils applying for jobs. Two other areas need some special mention.

Work experience

Many secondary schools have work experience schemes whereby pupils under the statutory leaving age have time off from school to have practical experience in working situations which can be of obvious benefit to them. This is permitted under the Education (Work Experience) Act 1973 and guidelines for such schemes are to be found in DFE Circular 7/74. Schools need to establish relationships and clear understandings with the employers concerned.

Points to note and check include the following:

1 Easter leavers may start work experience schemes at the end of the spring term of their fourth year. Summer leavers may start schemes on the day after the May school leaving date of their fourth year.
2 The LEA's regulations should be followed.
3 The scheme must be educational and not purely vocational. Employers must be aware of this and involved in the planning.
4 As far as possible, the experience should be related to work in school and preparatory work should be undertaken.
5 The experience should be linked to careers work in school.
6 Work experience should be available to pupils of all abilities.
7 It must be suitable and safe for those involved.
8 Employers must not make payments to pupils, schools or LEAs since this is illegal and may invalidate insurance contracts.
9 Employers must not use the schemes as means of assessment for future employment.
10 Pupils must not be charged for transport.
11 Parents should be given information and their consent obtained.
12 School staff should supervise pupils by visiting them on site.
13 The position over insurance needs to be clarified.

Part-time employment

What pupils do outside school is largely a matter for their parents but if outside conditions affect school work adversely then some action may be needed. The part-time employment of school pupils under the statutory leaving age may be a relevant factor.

Part-time employment is only permitted for those aged 13 or over. It is regulated by bye-laws made by local authorities and so details may vary from one area to another. Children must not work for more than two hours a day and not before 7 a.m. or after 7 p.m. They must not work in occupations which involve risks to health, safety or morals and the bye-laws usually name certain establishments which are expressly excluded, such as public houses, betting shops and those where intoxicating liquor is sold. Factories, quarries, ships, aircraft and underground mines are expressly forbidden. Whether payment is made or not is immaterial – the aim is to protect and prevent exploitation.

Enforcement of the law is, unfortunately, rarely undertaken. It is in the hands of local authorities and usually exercised through the education welfare service. There is a power to prosecute. Many owners of small businesses are genuinely unaware of the legislation and often, in the interests of good local relationships, a tactful approach by a school to parents or the employer may help, rather than a request for an official investigation. If schools do feel that official action is necessary then a check of local bye-laws should be made and the LEA informed.

Further reading

The Children Act itself is heavy going but HMSO has produced a simpler guide in its *Introduction to The Children Act*, 1989. Many authorities have produced their own guidelines for schools and education welfare officers. A useful general handbook is *Family Law and Practice* by Reekie and Tuddenham (1990), published by Sweet and Maxwell. *Criminal Law* by P. Seago (1989), also published by Sweet and Maxwell, gives a concise introduction to the subject.

Test yourself – External relations

1 What is meant by parental responsibility for a child?

2 Who may have parental responsibility?

3 Is the concept of parental responsibility helpful to schools?

4 Mary wants to go on a school trip and parental consent is necessary. In her case responsibility lies with mother, father and step-father. Who may give permission?

5 Mr A wants Jack withdrawn from lessons in RE but Mrs A does not. The matter reaches the Family Proceedings Court. Which order might it decide to make?

6 Simon lives with his mother in Devon and attends a local school. His estranged father, who now lives in Yorkshire, arrives at school unexpectedly and demands to see him. The head refuses since there is a suspicion that he intends to take Simon away. The mother, who has heard from a neighbour that the husband is in the area, calls at school to remove Simon. She is also refused. Has the head acted correctly?

7 A parent demands that her daughter be excused permanently from a particular physical activity. Does she have a right to insist?

8 A local shopkeeper has informed the police that pupils from a school are stealing from him. A constable arrives and asks to speak to certain pupils. What should the head do?

9 A school receives an anonymous letter alleging that Mr X is subjecting his child to physical violence at home. The head is reasonably sure that this is malicious and untrue. Should any action be taken?

10 Jack appears to be very tired in school and sometimes falls asleep in class. Apparently, he has an early morning paper round and another part-time job. What should his school do?

Comments will be found at the end of the book (page 212).

16 Data protection, defamation and copyright

These three areas all raise possible legal problems for schools in determining their organisation and conduct. They relate to the collection and storage of information relating to pupils, parents and staff; correspondence and interviews between teachers and parents and character and professional references; and the use of material in schools which may be the subject of copyright.

Data protection

Throughout this book there have been references to records that have to be kept and information to be stored – admission and attendance registers, results of testing under the National Curriculum, accident reports and so on. Clearly, schools need to establish careful arrangements over the gathering and storage of such material. This used to be done manually and there were few legal constraints on what took place. The use of computers, now common in most schools, has changed this, largely because of the possible abuses of privacy that are now present. The new law is based on the Data Protection Act of 1984. It is a criminal Act, so breach may result in prosecution.

The Act applies to all who control the storage of personal data by automatic means i.e. by computer or wordprocessor (storage by manual means is not covered) and it requires them to register as 'users'. An LEA will be a user and it is likely that the governing body and the head will also qualify, as indeed will any individual teacher who stores 'personal data' relating to pupils or their parents by automatic means. Personal data is defined as information about living, identifiable human beings.

Those who store such personal data are required to observe certain principles:

1 The information must be collected lawfully and fairly and the purpose must be made known to those affected by the process.

2 The purpose itself must be lawful and specified in the registration by the user.

3 The data must be relevant and not excessive for the purpose.

4 It must be accurate and kept up to date but retained for no longer than is necessary.

5 Individuals have a right to know if personal data is held concerning them, to be shown a copy on request and to have any errors corrected.

6 Users must take suitable steps over the security of the data that has been stored.

Who is the user?

The LEA will have to register as a user because it will need to store a mass of personal data. If a school is collecting data of a statistical nature for transmission to the DFE then it is acting as agent for the LEA and will be covered by its registration. If, however, a school is storing data as part of its duties imposed on the governors or the head, or for other internal purposes, then it will need to register as a user, either in the name of the governors or the head. Most schools will now need to do this.

What information may be stored?

Of course, any information may be stored but recent guidelines from the DFE suggest that if any of the following are included then registration as a user is necessary:

Area	User
Admission and attendance registers	Governors
Pupil curriculum records	"
Exemptions from the National Curriculum	"
Records of public examination entries	"
Staff records – except pay and pensions	"
Private school funds	"
Assessment under the National Curriculum	Head

Written reports to parents	"
Teaching materials	"
Staff appraisal	"
Pupil disciplinary records	"
Staff records – pay and pensions	LEA
School expenditure – delegated budget	"

Access

Under the Education (School Records) Regulations 1989, parents of pupils under 18 and pupils themselves over 16 have a right of access, with some limitations, to individual records held manually. The Data Protection Act gives right of access to the child or to the parent on behalf of the child. If the child understands the nature of the request then the information must be given to him or her, otherwise to the parent. The information must be in the interests of the child not the parent or the user may refuse access.

Exemptions

Full details of exemptions are available from the Registrar in Guidelines 6. They include a statement of a child's special educational needs, professional statements on the physical and mental health of an individual and information which would indicate someone other than the individual concerned.

Registration

LEAs will be able to offer advice but the registration is made through:

The Data Protection Registrar,
Springfield House,
Water Lane,
Wilmslow,
Cheshire SK9 5AX

from whom all definitive information is available.

Defamation

The right to free speech and free expression in writing is not absolute. Limitations are imposed by the criminal law concerning obscenity, threatening behaviour, incitement to racial hatred and so on. In civil law a limitation that may concern teachers and schools is that relating to the tort of defamation. Because of cases involving pop stars, politicians and other famous figures where large sums are awarded in compensation there may be an impression that actions in defamation are easy to pursue and likely to be profitable. In fact, bringing such an action is likely to be very costly (legal aid is not available in defamation cases), proof is difficult and the outcome unpredictable since juries are often used.

What is defamation?

Defamation is the making of a false statement about another which tends to lower that person's reputation in the eyes of ordinary, decent citizens. The defamatory statement must be published – that is, communicated to a third party – and it must be reasonably clear that the statement refers to the person making the complaint.

If a person has been convicted of theft and is then referred to as a thief that is not defamatory since the statement is not false. However, to call a child a thief in front of others is certainly capable of being defamatory until a conviction has been brought about. For a parent to accuse a teacher of being over-zealous in disciplinary matters would not be defamatory – many ordinary people would approve. A parent who, in the privacy of a study, calls a head a liar cannot be sued – the statement has not been published. This situation would be different if another member of staff were present or a communicating door were open so that a secretary heard what had been said. If both parents were present this would make no difference – statements from husband to wife and vice versa do not amount to publication. A parent who stated that teachers on a staff of 70 were incompetent could not be sued since it would be impossible to prove direct reference to individuals; the position would be quite different if only two or three staff were concerned.

The judge in an action decides whether a statement is capable of being defamatory and the jury decides on the facts whether indeed it was so.

Slander and libel

Defamation may be in the form of slander or libel. Slander is defamation in a transient form, speech or even gesture. It is normally only actionable if the complainant can show that the publication of the statement actually caused him or her some harm. Teachers enjoy an exception here. If the slander relates to a person's professional competence then no special damage has to be proved, the assumption being that it must be damaging. A further exception is that of a statement alleging that a woman is unchaste; parents or others alleging sexual misbehaviour on the part of a woman teacher may be sued without proof of special damage and staff questioning senior girl pupils need to choose their words carefully. There are no such exceptions for males.

Libel is defamation in a permanent form. This is frequently in writing but a tape or video recording certainly may constitute libel and so may a painting or drawing. It does not matter that the statement could easily be removed – writing on a blackboard, for example, would be libellous. The difference between libel and slander is important because libel is actionable *per se* – that is, no special damage has to be proved. If the complainant's reputation has been lowered in the minds of decent people then that is enough.

Remedies and defences

A person bringing an action in defamation will go either to the County Court or the High Court and will seek a court injunction to prevent further repetition of the defamation and may seek compensation in the form of money damages for the harm suffered. The award may be a large sum, as in some sensational cases, or it may be only nominal. To bring such an action is a gamble for ordinary people and teachers need union advice and backing before becoming involved. A warning letter may well have the desired effect.

There are a number of defences available. The obvious one is justification, i.e. that the statement is true. For teachers the defence of qualified privilege may apply. This is possible where there is some obligation or duty to comment, as in a teacher reporting on a pupil or a head or LEA writing a report or reference on an employee. If in the process a defamatory statement is published the complainant must show that it was made out of spite, malice or gross negligence. A genuine mistake is not actionable though, of course, those who write reports should take care to be accurate. Parents criticising the performance of governors, heads or staff may have the defence of fair comment on a matter of public interest if the statement is one of genuine criticism and not made out of malice or spite. It must be a statement of opinion, not of fact. Except for statements by the media, an apology is not strictly a defence but it does show evidence of regret and an effort to remedy matters. It may thus lead to a reduction in the amount of any damages awarded.

Davy Jones

We can now relate the law concerning defamation to a letter written to the head by Davy's father.

Seaview,
Beach Road,
Stormhaven.

Dear Head,

I am very dissatisfied with what goes on at your school and your treatment of my son, Davy. You punished him severely for being found behind the bike shed with his girl friend where nothing wrong took place. His teacher, Miss Calypso, who from all accounts is nothing but a vindictive bitch, called him a little bastard in front of his mates and then threw him out of the class for no reason at all. He has been given a disgusting history book on World War 1 which contains swear words used by troops in the trenches. From all this it is obvious that you are not a fit person to run a school and that you cannot control your staff who seem to be a load of useless lefties.

I am sending a copy of this letter to your employers and taking legal advice.

Yours,

A. B. Jones

Mr Jones has certainly made statements here which could be defamatory in the form of libel since they are in writing. He has stated that the head is professionally incompetent and made similar references to the teaching staff. His comment on Miss Calypso would certainly lower her reputation in the eyes of other ordinary people. If he has sent a copy of his letter to the LEA or to governors then the material has been published to a third party and in the case of the head and Miss Calypso the statements clearly refer to them.

Does Mr Jones have any defences? Unless he can justify his comments he can only rely on his right to make fair comment. Those on the use of the history book could be acceptable, so, possibly, could his criticism of the school – if couched in less emotive language. But his statement of fact of the head's incompetence is actionable. There is no defence of his description of Miss Calypso as a vindictive bitch with its connotations of spite and possible sexual innuendo. Even if he does not send a copy of his letter to others Miss Calypso may take action – his statement has been published to the head. Similarly, the reference to other staff has been published but it is not precise enough for individuals to take action.

If Mr Jones gets good legal advice it is likely to be to do nothing. However, he might have grounds for an action if Davy has indeed been called a bastard in front of other pupils. Normally, what is termed 'mere vulgar abuse' does not amount to defamation – slander in this case – but if Miss Calypso has used the word and a court is satisfied that pupils understood this to imply that Davy was illegitimate then action might be possible. It seems unlikely.

Copyright

In law, copyright is a form of intellectual property. That is it consists not of something tangible but of a right to exert control by taking action in court. Perhaps the best example of such property is that of a debt where the creditor has a right to sue for the amount due or assign the right to collect or sue to another. The essence of copyright is that the owner, who may not be the original creator, has the right to decide on the use of the material that is protected.

Copyright is automatic – there is no need to register or declare it. It does not lie in the original idea itself but in the form in which that idea is given substance. Someone who expresses an idea for a story has not created copyright until the story is written or recorded in some other way. A second person could take the idea and write his or her own story, thus creating copyright. Copyright exists in any creation which has an element of originality about it – the copying of ordinary routine information which is readily available is not covered though the way in which it is presented might be.

Copyright normally lies with the creator, whether this is a famous author or a pupil drawing a cartoon for a school magazine. Like all other property, it may be sold or left by will. An increasing practice, particularly with language tapes, is to waive copyright but include an extra sum for this in the initial charge. One exception to ownership may affect teachers. If an employee is required to produce material as part of the duties for which payment is made then copyright may well lie with the employer unless an agreement otherwise has been made. Teachers producing materials with a view to publication should be careful to do this outside school hours and using their own equipment and materials.

The remedies for breach of copyright are a court injunction forbidding repetition of the infringement and a claim for money damages as compensation.

The law of copyright has always been complex and difficult to apply. This has become increasingly so with the introduction of tape and video recording and the use of computers. The existing law is to be found in the Copyright, Designs and Patents Act 1988 which applies throughout the UK and which sets up a Copyright Tribunal to deal with disputes and thus prevent excessive court action; a snag is that the earlier law may still apply to works created before that date. Checking with the owner is always advisable if there is any doubt.

Even establishing who that owner is may prove difficult since one particular work may involve a number of owners. Even with a book there will be at least two owners – the author and the publishers who own copyright of the typeface. With a musical recording there may be the composer, the lyricist, the vocalist and musicians and the company which made the recording.

What is covered?

As far as schools are concerned the law covers:

1. Original literary, dramatic, musical and artistic works
2. Sound recordings, films, broadcasts and cable programmes
3. Typographical arrangements for published editions

All this means that books used throughout a school are included, so are plays used for rehearsing productions, so is the music used in class and for concerts and so are paintings and drawings used in lessons or for display. Even if the copyright of the creator has expired long ago – with Shakespeare, for example – then it may still exist in a published edition. Tapes, CDs and video cassettes are included and so are radio and television broadcasts.

Put simply, the copyright lasts for 50 years from the end of the calendar year in which the creator dies or, if the author is unknown, 50 years from the date at which the work was created. Copyright of published editions expires after 25 years.

All this means that schools have to be careful over the use of copyright material and there have been several actions against schools in recent years because of infringements. Fortunately, there are ways in which the problems may be eased.

Permitted copying

The Act allows a number of exceptions to the rules. Those that are of significance for schools include:

1. A relatively insignificant element of a large work. A page of a novel could be copied but not four lines of a sonnet.
2. A reasonable proportion of a published work or journal for individual research or study, either personally or by a library. What is 'reasonable' is not clear.
3. Fair dealing – copies made for research or private study.
4. Making single copies for instruction e.g. for use on an OHP.
5. Playing of films, broadcasts, cable programmes or sound recordings as part of instruction.
6. For examination purposes (not including music).
7. Public recitation, if suitably acknowledged.
8. Where reasonable efforts to find the owner have failed and the work seems to be out of copyright.
9. When permitted by licence.

Licensing

Attempts have been made to regularise copying by the setting up of licensing agencies. Two of these are of concern to schools:

The Copyright Licensing Agency

Most LEAs are registered with this Agency and this allows their schools to carry out copying by mechanical and electronic means under the agreement. Other schools may join. Up to 5% of any work registered with the CLA may be copied and most major publishers are members. Under the licence schools should display a notice beside machines giving details of the scheme and the limitations on copying which apply. Licensing with this Agency does not cover music.

The Educational Recording Agency

This body came into being as a direct result of the 1988 Act. From May 1990 all educational establishments were required to take out a licence if they wished to record programmes. Schools pay a single annual fee and are then allowed to copy any TV or radio programmes made by members of ERA. These include the BBC, ITV and Channel 4 but not the Open University.

Further reading

Guidelines on data protection may be obtained from the Registrar at the address given on page 189. Further discussion of defamation will be found in any standard work on Law of Tort. A *Copyright Clearance Guide* is published by the National Council for Educational Technology at 3, Devonshire Street, London W1N 2BA and details of licensing may be obtained from the two Agencies, which are both at 33/34 Alfred Place, London WC1E 7DP.

Test yourself – comments

The new governors (page 29)

1 The answer will be set out clearly in your Instrument. It should be noted that the individual governors are not delegates. They may reflect their own views as well as those of others and the way they vote is entirely a matter for themselves. LEA, foundation and minor authority governors may be removed by the body which appointed them – others must be allowed to complete their term of office.

2 Again, the answers are in the Instrument. There must always be a termly meeting plus such others as the governors themselves decide. Only a meeting that is quorate may make a binding decision. Notice of seven days is the norm.

3 Governors' meetings are private though they may invite anyone else to attend if they wish. Such persons may be allowed to speak but they must not vote. The minutes are not private. Once approved by the next meeting and signed by the chair they must be available for public inspection at the school. The exception is for any item considered to be confidential – usually items related to individual members of staff, named pupils or problem families. The LEA may declare an item to be confidential but otherwise the chair decides whether any matter shall be confidential and the record of such a matter is not open to public scrutiny.

4 It is unlikely that your Instrument provides an answer as yet though eventually it will do so. There may be as many committees as the governors wish but if they are to have fully delegated powers then they must be properly constituted and must not be contrary to the Education (School Government) Regulations 1989 mentioned above. Neither the head nor a teacher governor may be chair of such a committee.

5 Your Articles should contain references to the LEA, the governors and the National Curriculum as well as reference to religious education. The governors decide on whether sex education shall be included and the form it shall take, though it must have due regard for morals and family life. Have yours made any decisions in this matter?

6 When the Articles are fully updated according to LMS they will show the power of the governors to appoint, discipline and dismiss staff. Although the LEA are the employers in the case of county and voluntary controlled schools they must still go along with the decisions of governors unless they can show that the latter have acted unreasonably or unfairly.

7 The Articles allow the governors to make a statement of general policy over pupil discipline and to give specific instructions over particular points. Have yours done this? Otherwise discipline, the setting and maintaining of standards of behaviour and the rules for pupils are matters for the head.

8 The Articles yet again. They will set out the cumbersome procedure to be followed. Governors cannot exclude – only the head may do that. Governors must hear appeals and may order the head to re-admit. They may well become involved later with the LEA and the local appeals committee.

9 There will be a section in the Articles under finance. Providing the governors act within their budget and the law they may spend their allocation as they wish. The overall budget must be approved by the full governing body and there must be proper accounting and auditing. The LEA may take over finance if malpractice or incompetence occurs.

10 These can be very complicated but the arrangements should be clarified in your Articles. They are based upon a 'standard number' which is calculated in different ways for primary and secondary schools. To make matters worse there are different arrangements for county and voluntary controlled schools as compared with voluntary aided and special agreement schools. The LEA and governors must consult annually over the arrangements and the proposed admission number for each school must be stated together with any criteria for selection to be used if a school is oversubscribed.

Test yourself – comments

The Contract of service (page 60)

1 The contract is binding when acceptance is given to a clear offer from the employer. This may be oral but is more likely to be in writing. Governing bodies of voluntary aided, grant maintained schools and city technology colleges are the employer, otherwise it is the LEA. In independent schools the employer may be the individual owner, trustees or a board of directors. Acceptance by post is complete on posting.

2 Within 13 weeks of appointment a teacher must be given details of the job title, salary, conditions of service, sickness and injury benefit, pension rights, disciplinary and grievance procedures and notice to be given by either side. If full details are not actually given, as with conditions of service, then reference must be made to the appropriate document.

3 Conditions of service are to be found in the *Burgundy* and *Blue Books* plus any other items issued by the employer, though these must not be contrary to law. No, the conditions are not definitive. They are express terms certainly but other terms may be implied as a result of test cases in the courts.

4 Miss Pretty is in breach of contract and should be told so but the school is virtually helpless. An action for breach of contract is open but hardly worthwhile and the courts will not enforce performance of the contract by Miss Pretty. At some time in the future, when the glamour has faded perhaps, she may want a reference but the school is then under no obligation to give one.

5 Rollasurface will be independent contractors and vicariously liable for the negligence of their employees. The teacher's employer is vicariously liable for his or her negligence also. If Rollasurface had made a condition that pupils should not be

allowed on the playground while work was in progress then the negligence is the teacher's. Otherwise, the injured pupil may sue the firm and the teacher's employer severally or jointly with the court apportioning damages as it sees fit.

6 Vicarious liability is the principle whereby an employer is liable for the torts (civil wrongs) of employees acting within their course of employment. The employer may then sue the employee but is more likely to take disciplinary action.

7 When carrying out duties clearly connected with the employment or which have been authorised by the employer of his agent. Some LEAs, while providing insurance cover for extra-curricular activities, maintain that such voluntary activities are not within the course of employment. Based on cases outside teaching, the writer believes this to be an incorrect interpretation of the law.

8 No, warnings are not essential but they are highly desirable since they provide evidence of the employer's fairness in giving an employee every chance of putting things right. Certainly, for gross misconduct no warning may be necessary before dismissal. The form is a matter for the employer but it would be wise to follow the guidelines of ACAS and/or agreements with teacher unions.

9 Not true. If the tribunal decides that the dismissal was fair then the teacher gets nothing. If the dismissal was unfair then compensation is granted though even this may be reduced if the teacher has contributed significantly to the stated cause. If the tribunal orders re-instatement the employer may refuse, in which case additional compensation is awarded.

10 Redundancy is a form of dismissal so the law relating to unfair dismissal applies. If there are agreed procedures over redundancy then they must be followed to ensure fairness. Otherwise, guidelines similar to those suggested towards the end of Chapter 6 should be devised.

Test yourself – comments

Appointments, pay and conditions (page 90)

1 Yes. To advertise for a mistress to teach history is discrimination against male applicants. To advertise for a PE mistress could be justified in any school on grounds of decency and privacy under the legislation.

2 The governors of a voluntary aided school are the employers and so they may make a firm offer. If this is accepted then the contract is complete. Such agreements do not have to be in writing but it is always wise to confirm them in this way.

3 Yes, she can. S.30(9) of the *Blue Book* requires a head to provide information regarding the work and performance of staff where this is relevant to their future employment.

4 Well, it is not an unlawful one but one, like those relating to politics or religious beliefs in a non-denominational school, best avoided. For most schools, where the head lives and how he or she gets to work is a personal matter as long as duties are carried out satisfactorily. The era of tied school houses is over.

5 There are ways. Progression up the standard scale could be accelerated by one point or payment at an incremental point could be enhanced as long as it was still below the next point on the scale. If the teacher is already at the top of the scale then governors have discretion to extend it.

6 Mrs D is entitled to have her job back but she may be asked to carry out any duties reasonably covered by her contract. The head could make reasonable changes to the duties of any teacher during a school year. If she was appointed specifically as an English specialist with a clear promise of GCSE work then she has a case. It is

more likely that she was appointed as an English teacher but with the statement that she carries out such other duties as are reasonable. If her qualifications include geography then she has no case unless her allocation of English periods is an obvious token gesture. Certainly, on return she is not entitled to a replica of her original timetable – the circumstances may well have changed.

7 Mr E is in breach of contract. Disciplinary action could be taken and pay deducted. A simple phone call to the head could probably have put matters right since extended compassionate leave is permissible, with a request put in writing after the crisis is over.

8 Probably not, though it is foolish not to do so. Who knows what may happen during an eventful school year – and someone may be keeping a log. A statement of directed time is clear evidence of planning and an awareness of the rights of staff.

9 Yes, she must. This is required under S.35(4) of the *Blue Book* and is a compulsory element in Mrs F's contract of service. If she is adamant in refusing then she is in breach of contract and may be dismissed. If she chooses to resign there will be no compensation. However, the situation seems to be a sad reflection on how appraisal has been explained to her. Handled tactfully its merits and safeguards could hardly be a threat to her dignity, indeed appraisal would reflect the value of all the service she gives.

10 This sounds unreasonable. Some heads seem obsessed with the minutiae of the dress of pupils and staff. Providing a teacher presents herself or himself dressed in a clean and reasonably normal manner then the employer has no right to dictate over detail. The real difficulty here lies in the use of 'directed'. This is more likely to raise hackles than lower skirts. The reason behind the instruction may well be that some female members of staff are having disciplinary problems and not realising one of the causes. This is no reason to annoy those competent teachers who have firm control, mini-skirted or not. The message could have been handled better by substituting 'requested' for 'directed' but written messages tend to have an authoritarian air. A senior female member of staff could well be asked to counsel those having problems with discipline.

Test yourself – comments

Managing pupils (page 130)

1 There is no British case on this particular point but an Australian one, which is not binding on our courts, declared that teachers must act as good responsible parents, not the parents of the particular pupil. To this must be added the concept of the parent who has had the benefit of professional teacher training. Any other interpretation would be impossible since teachers would have to behave differently towards each pupil. Tommy Atkins may be lucky. His parents may be quite irresponsible but his teacher must not be so. Equally, over-protective parents cannot expect teachers to behave in the same way.

2 Richard's parents must prove a duty of care owed, breach of that duty and damage that was reasonably foreseeable. The facts here are similar to those in *Mays v Essex C.C. 1975*. The judge refused to find any negligence. A duty of care existed and damage which was, perhaps, foreseeable. He did not find breach, however, declaring that good parents would allow their children to enjoy the thrill of sliding on ice. He added that sliding in this way was every schoolboy's right – he made no reference to girls! The answer might well have been different if Richard had slipped on untreated ice at the entrance to his school.

3 If you consent to run a risk you cannot then sue for the consequences that might reasonably be expected from taking that risk. Thus, all who take part in sports or games consent to the risks involved. By sending pupils to school parental consent is implied to all the hazards normally associated with school life, on playgrounds and sports fields for example. Where particular risks on an extra-curricular activity are made clear to parents then, by agreeing to participation, they have consented to those being taken.

4 In a number of cases judges have repeated that continuous supervision of pupils cannot reasonably be expected in many school situations but all supervision must be adequate in the light of particular circumstances. So, supervision on playgrounds need not be continuous but it should certainly be so in a workshop full of dangerous machines.

5 Normally, pupils are only covered by insurance if their injuries are the result of negligence on the part of an employer, either because of defects in premises or equipment or negligent conduct of staff. Thus, a child injured at school by a sheer accident will receive no compensation. Personal accident insurance would cover this but usually it is left to parents to take this out. It would cover pupils for injuries both at school and outside.

6 No. Figures are often quoted from LEA regulations, union statements or DFE publications but they have no strict legal basis. The law requires supervision to be reasonable according to the circumstances and it could well be that a local authority's regulations were held to be inadequate. However, they should be followed since that is evidence of reasonable care on the part of the school. A head who believes them to be unsatisfactory is free to make better provision.

7 Mrs F was wrong. Responsibility for pupils may end at a school's boundary, unless pupils are in the care of staff, but case law supports the right to enforce school rules off the premises, certainly when pupils are on the way to and from school.

8 Reasonable force may be used when pupils are creating a danger to themselves, to others or to property. S.47(3) of the 1986 (No.2) Act makes it clear that this does not amount to corporal punishment. The force used must be reasonable.

9 A person who takes responsibility for the property of another may be liable if that property is lost, misused or damaged. This incident raises an interesting point. It constitutes a tort, a form of trespass to goods, and an employer is vicariously liable for the torts of employees. The employer might be liable for the loss of the watch. The bringing of watches could be banned but that seems unreasonable in the case of senior pupils. A disclaimer might help, i.e. that if watches are worn a school will take no responsibility for them – though some form of checking system would seem advisable for PE lessons.

10 The head cannot authorise re-admission, though that will come automatically if the period of exclusion has been for a stated period. The governors may authorise it. In the case of county and controlled schools the LEA may do so. For these and aided schools the independent appeals panel may take such action.

Test yourself – comments

The school and parents (page 133)

1 Of course, we do not know what has taken place at the meetings Mrs Toogood has had with various members of staff. She may have been given a fair hearing, her complaints listened to and action taken, if that were possible. She may have been treated dismissively or fobbed off with vague platitudes.

If the complaints are justified then some parental rights may well have been ignored. Mr and Mrs Toogood have a right to full information regarding the school. They are entitled to inspect syllabuses of work. There is a right to withdraw Amanda from lessons in RE. Any test results for her under the National Curriculum must be made available to them. The means of making complaints must also be made known.

If they have received a prospectus containing all this information then their complaints relating to these matters are unjustified – otherwise the school is at fault.

Also, they have a right to choose a school. If they are so unhappy about Faraway then Amanda can be transferred to another school which has a spare place, or even educated at home.

Certain issues they raise give them no rights. Amanda must study the subjects laid down in the National Curriculum, plus others decided upon by the school, unless she is in the special needs category and that does not appear to be so. School governors decide upon the policy over sex education and Mr and Mrs Toogood must go along with that policy. PE is a part of the curriculum and Amanda must participate unless declared unfit on medical evidence. The school can insist on an examination if necessary. The Toogoods must comply with reasonable school rules.

The rather wild accusations of bullying, victimisation and staff incompetence are open questions but not perhaps insignificant.

2 Although the Toogoods are difficult parents and one suspects a strained domestic situation – demanding father impatient with mother and daughter perhaps – the school's handling of the incident is open to some criticism.

When visitors arrive at a school the first impression given is of paramount importance. It needs to be one of welcome and pleasant efficiency. The attitude of reception staff is crucial since their performance may well be responsible for the tone of what is to follow. Here the Toogoods have been forced to wait (perhaps unavoidably) but there seems to have been no apology and no offer of a seat. The suggestion is then given of a barrier keeping them from the head and again directing them to other staff. 'Perhaps the head is afraid,' thinks Mr Toogood.

When the head does become involved the situation is almost out of hand. Perhaps if he had allowed the parents to air their frustrations without an angry reaction, noted their complaints, produced a prospectus, sent for Amanda's file (we assume one exists) and acknowledged at least one right – that of withdrawal from RE – then all might not have been lost. If specific instances of bullying or victimisation could have been identified then an investigation could have been promised and a further appointment made. A cup of tea might have helped.

3 There are at least four.

a The reception given to visitors needs to be assessed. Reception staff are busy people dealing with phone calls, notes, forgotten sandwiches and PE kit and a score of other items but they must be aware of their importance as the first personal contact visitors make with a school.

b Information relating to individual pupils must be readily available to those dealing with visiting parents. Faraway needs to examine its arrangements over this.

c Heads and senior staff need to have strategies for putting parents at their ease so that discussion can take place in a constructive way for the benefit of everyone, particularly the pupils. Comfortable seating, a knowledge of the individual pupil, a willingness to listen before stating the school's position and an awareness of parental anxieties are all important. Given these, staff can then be tactful but firm.

d Even comments from parents which on the surface seem to be unreasonable or unjustified merit some serious consideration. Perhaps there is a deal of bullying going on which is condoned or unnoticed by staff. Perhaps a particular teacher is treating pupils in a way that is unacceptable. Perhaps Mrs Toogood has not been treated reasonably at earlier interviews. The head needs to find out and take any action needed.

Test yourself – comments

Safety, premises and transport (page 158)

1 False. Offenders may be prosecuted but the main purpose is to encourage employers to be alive to risks and take reasonable steps to guard against them.

2 A Regulation is mandatory but a Code of Practice is not. However, failure to follow a Code could amount to not acting reasonably.

3 The responsibility lies with the employer. If the head or member of staff has deliberately ignored instructions, or acted in a grossly negligent way, then they might be prosecuted and would be liable to discipline by the employer. The safety representative has no legal responsibility – a moral one certainly.

4 The head should record the accident and complete a report for the employer and the Health and Safety inspectorate since this is clearly a 'dangerous occurrence'. It may not be possible to change exits, roads and car parks, but have speed ramps and crash barriers been considered? The head should also see that pupils are warned regularly of the dangers and staff are reminded of the need to drive slowly. A member of staff failing to cooperate could be banned from bringing a car onto the premises.

5 The inspector could issue a prohibition notice banning the use of the exits or of the road alongside but this is most unlikely. An improvement notice could be issued requiring action to be taken over the provision of warning notices, speed ramps or crash barriers.

6 The unions have a right to nominate any employee as their safety representative and the head cannot refuse to accept that nomination and must cooperate with Mr Redman. If, however, he does not perform his duties satisfactorily then the head must complain to the unions that have appointed him.

7 Specialists who work on school premises are expected to cope with hazards normally incurred in their occupation. The window cleaner would have no redress unless the fall was due to a serious defect in the building which he could not have discovered by reasonable care. There would be liability to the first parent who is on the premises for a lawful purpose and the occupier owes him a common duty of care. The dangerous state of the seat breaks that duty. Unless a settlement was made he would have an action in negligence. The second parent has exceeded the permission given to enter the building. He has not been authorised to use machines so there is no liability.

8 Liability to trespassers is normally limited to not creating dangers for them. However, where trespassing is known or can easily be foreseen care must be taken to limit the impact of potential hazards and this is particularly so in relation to child trespassers. Here a warning notice has been displayed and the gates locked. These should be sufficient deterrents to older youngsters capable of understanding their significance, even if the open window might be an attraction. The injury to a trespasser by a faulty gas appliance could hardly have been foreseen anyway. Note, however, that a similar injury to a canteen assistant would be a breach of safety and one to a PTA member heating milk for a coffee evening would be a breach of the occupier's duty of care.

9 Except for HMI, governors, officers of the local authority, meter readers and so on the head may declare anyone a trespasser and ask them to leave the premises. That includes suspended staff and excluded pupils and certainly parents. If they fail to leave and create a nuisance or disturbance then they commit an offence under S.40 of the Local Government (Miscellaneous Provisions) Act 1982. The head needs to declare Mr X a trespasser and require him to leave. If he refuses then the head may use reasonable force to eject him (not advisable). The police may be called and they may use reasonable force to remove him (a better solution). A prosecution might then follow. Readers may query 'creating a nuisance or disturbance' here. Mr X does not even have to

threaten or abuse – his continuing presence creates the nuisance and magistrates have been known to impose fines where only passive defiance was involved.

10 The head must see that a licence for public entertainment has been applied for and granted and that all its conditions are met relating to seating, exits, lighting and fire-fighting equipment. The licence for the bar may be obtained by a representative of the PTA though the head may need to ensure that this is done. A raffle held internally on the evening needs no permission.

Test yourself – comments

External relations (page 185)

1 The concept of parental responsibility replaces the old notion of custody. Parental responsibility means a duty to have practical concern for the welfare and upbringing of a child.

2 Anyone. Natural parents receive it automatically and so do step-parents and adoptive parents. Others may be granted it by the Family Proceedings Court. If there is no-one else to take it then the local authority must do so.

3 Yes and no. It should help to clarify legal rights and responsibilities in relation to split families. On the other hand, all with responsibility are entitled to rights over information, consultation and so on.

4 The new law does not seem to have clarified this position but to obtain permission from each seems too cumbersome. A school would be safe in obtaining consent from any one of them. However, it is suggested that if another one raised a serious objection then Mary should not be allowed to go.

5 A specific issue order.

6 This illustrates the need for a school to know the terms of residence and access relating to various members of the family. The father here is unlikely to have right of residence for Simon and his access will have been laid down by the court. It is most unlikely to be at any time so the head's refusal is probably justified though the father could be given information regarding Simon's work and progress. If the mother has right of residence then it is suggested that she does have power to remove him in the short term and it is wrong to refuse her.

7 Only if there is a clear statement from the doctor, or from the School Medical Officer, that the excusal is necessary on medical grounds.

8 Refuse and point out that the pupils should be interviewed at home in the presence of parents. If the police insist do not obstruct them but insist on being present and then report the incident, giving the constable's number.

9 Yes. The head cannot be sure. Social Services and/or the N.S.P.C.C. need to be informed – the head could say that the allegation was likely to be malicious. A discreet eye should then be kept on the child for any signs of possible abuse.

10 If Jack is under 13 he should not be working at all. Even if he is older then he may only work for two hours a day and not before seven in the morning or after seven at night. The two jobs are likely to break those conditions. His parents need to be aware of the effect on his behaviour in school. If matters are not put right then the education welfare officer needs to be involved, rather than an approach made to the employers.

Useful addresses

Advisory Centre for Education, 18 Victoria Park Square, London E2 9PB

Assistant Masters and Mistresses Association, 7 Nothumberland Street, London WC2N 5DA

Association of British Travel Agents, 55–57 Newman Street, London W1P 4AH

Association for Science Education, College Lane, Hatfield, Herts AL10 9AA

Automobile Association, Fanum House, Basingstoke, Hants RG21 2EA

Catholic Education Services, 41 Cromwell Road, London SW7 2DH

Charity Commissioners, St Alban's House, 57–60 Haymarket

Advisory Conciliation and Arbitration Services (ACAS), Clifton House, 83–117 Euston Road, London SW1Y 4QX

Commission for Racial Equality, Elliot House, 10–12 Allington Street, London SW1E 5EH

Council for Educational Technology, 3 Devonshire Street, London W1N 2BA

Curriculum Council for Wales, Suite 2, Castle Buildings,Womanby Street, Cardiff, CF1 9SX

The Data Protection Registrar, Springfield House, Water Lane, Wilmslow, Cheshire SK9 5AX

Department for Education, Sanctuary Buildings, Great Smith Street, Westminster, London SW1P 3BT

Department for Education, Pensions and Salaries Branch, Mowden Hall, Staindrop Road, Darlington, Co. Durham DL3 9BG

Department for Education, Publications Despatch Centre, Honeypot Lane, Stanmore, Middlesex HA7 1AZ

Driver and Vehicle Licensing Centre, Swansea SA99 1AB

Educational Recording Agency Ltd, 33–34 Alfred Place, London WC1E 7DP

Employment Appeal Tribunal, 4 St James's Square, London SW1Y 4JU

Equal Opportunities Commission, Overseas House, Quay Street, Manchester M3 3HN

General Synod Board of Education, Church House, Great Smith Street, London SW1P 3NZ

Grant Maintained Schools Centre, Wesley Court, 4a Priory Road, High Wycombe, Bucks HP13 6SE

Health and Safety Executive, St Hugh's House, Stanley Precinct, Bootle, Merseyside L20 3QZ

Her Majesty's Stationery Office, Publications Centre, PO Box 276, London SW8 5DT

Independent Schools Information Service, 56 Buckingham Gate, London SW1E 6AG

National Association of Governors and Managers, Christopher Hatton Centre, 26 Ladystall Street, London EC1R 4PQ

National Association of Head Teachers, 1 Heath Square, Boltro Road, Haywards Heath, West Sussex RH16 1BL

National Association of Schoolmasters/Union of Women Teachers, Educational Centre, Hillscourt, Rose Hill, Rednal, Birmingham B45 8RS

National Confederation of Parent-Teacher Associations, 43, Stonebridge Road, Gravesend, Kent DA11 9DZ

National Curriculum Council, Albion Wharf, 25 Skeldergate, York YO1 2XL

NSPCC, 67 Saffron Hill, London EC1N 8RS

National Union of Teachers, Hamilton House, Mabledon Place, London WC1H 9BD

Open University, Milton Keynes MK7 6AG

Professional Association of Teachers, 2 St James Court, Friargate, Derby DE1 1BT

Royal Automobile Club, PO Box 100, RAC House, Bartlett Street, South Croydon CR2 6XW

Safety and First Aid, 59 Hill Street, Liverpool L8 5SA

School Examinations and Assessment Council, Newcombe House, 45 Notting Hill Gate, London W11 3JB

School Journey Association of London, 48 Cavendish Road, London SW12 0DG

Scottish Education Department, New St Andrew's House, Edinburgh EH1 3TB

Secondary Heads Association, 130 Regent Road, Leicester LE1 7PG

Universities Central Council on Admissions, PO Box 28, Cheltenham, Gloucestershire GL50 3SA

Index